Interactive Optical Technologies in Education and Training:

Markets and Trends

Supplements to
Optical Information Systems

Interactive Optical Technologies in Education and Training:

Markets and Trends

SANDRA K. HELSEL

Meckler
Westport • London

Library of Congress Cataloging-in-Publication Data

Helsel, Sandra K.
    Interactive optical technologies in education and training :
    markets and trends / Sandra K. Helsel.
        p. cm. -- (Supplements to Optical information systems ; 8)
    Includes bibliographical references.
    ISBN 0-88736-392-X (alk. paper) : $
        1. Educational technology industries. 2. Instructional materials
    industry. 3. Audio-visual equipment industry. 4. Computer
    industry. 5. Market surveys.   I. Title.   II. Series: Supplement to
    Optical information systems ; 8.
    HD9811.A2H45   1990
    381'.45658312404--dc20   89-13521
                                                                              CIP

British Library Cataloguing in Publication Data

Helsel, Sandra K.
    Interactive optical technologies in education and
    training: markets and trends. - (Supplements to optical
    information systems; V. 8)
    1. Education. Applications of optical information
    retrieval systems
    I. Title II. Series
    370 ' .28 ' 5

    ISBN 0-88736-392-X

Meckler Corporation, 11 Ferry Lane West, Westport, CT 06880.
Meckler Ltd., Grosvenor Gardens House, Grosvenor Gardens,
    London SW1W 0BS, U.K.

Printed on acid free paper.
Printed and bound in the United States of America.

Contents

Foreword

I n use since the late 1970s in government, private industry, and education from kindergarten through graduate school, interactive optical technology has made an impressive impact on the computer, entertainment, and information markets. Increasingly, it is self-evident that the 1990s will be the decade in which the microcomputer becomes a basic multimedia environment in both the home and business markets.

Technology is now in place that will allow the storage of virtually any information format—still color image, full-motion video, machine-readable text, digital audio—on an optical disk. It is inevitable that the vision of merging print, audio, and video in an integrated computer/telecommunications/television system will become reality by the next century.

There are daily announcements that reflect the steady drive toward this vision. In 1989 and 1990, IBM announced new multimedia hardware and software tools for the PS/2 microcomputer series, and significant discounts off the retail price of its PS/2 and RT systems for educational institutions from kindergarten through graduate school. IBM, Philips, Microsoft, Sony, Pioneer, Intel, Lotus, Lockheed, and Xerox are just a few of the multinational firms involved in developing and implementing optical media products and systems.

Other vital signs indicate the rapid maturing of interactive optical technologies. One such sign is the formation of two new trade associations: the Interactive Video Industry Association (IVIA) and the Optical Publishing Association (OPA). Each group has independently announced its focus on the creation of standards, fostering new business ventures and opportunities, and public education awareness.

Many critical technological and market developments must occur before this vision becomes reality. Data interchange standards, analog-to-digital conversion technologies, true device portability, compact high-resolution displays including HDTV, laptop computers functionally comparable to dedicated workstations, connectivity, and systems integration are just some of the market and technical challenges facing companies investing in the development of optical media products.

We now know that users of computer-based information-management systems prefer those that offer such characteristics as portability, transparency, easy-to-use computers, and disk interchange-ability. During 1989, one of the first products based on Alan Kay's Dynabook concept was introduced using CD-ROM technology. The rewritable optical disk has caused considerable excitement and gained swift acceptance by hundreds of early adopters and system integrators. Developments continue in extension of natural language query, expert systems, and artificial intelligence. Impressive leaps and bounds are occurring in the laptop computer market. And our ability to digitize color images and typical office documents including handwritten items are goals being pursued by a growing number of firms. All of these developments reflect a commitment to the creation of our multimedia future.

Since optical storage is the medium of choice for the multimedia information and entertainment system of the future, it is remarkable that books published about the medium focus only on a specific format such as CD-ROM or interactive videodisc. In order for true market and product development to occur, an understanding of what is happening across the broad range of optical formats in areas such as education and training is essential. It is virtually impossible to plan and develop without an in-depth understanding of the trends in current usage of interactive optical technologies across the board.

This is an important book. It is the first that examines and explores the various educational and training uses of optical media. For the first time, individuals involved with optical media can now compare and contrast the various applications and uses of all interactive optical formats: interactive videodisc, CD-ROM, CD-ROM/XA, CD-I, and DVI. Investigating current usage and development trends of interactive optical technologies will be instructive for both the product developer and end-user.

This is a timely book for product and market developers as well as current and prospective users of optical-based, interactive information systems. As we start the new decade, there will be confusion concerning which optical media format to choose for the delivery of information in the home and business. This will also be a challenging time for end-users who must make informed purchase decisions that will meet both long- and short-term needs.

Technologically, we are living in exciting times. Interactive optical technologies test our ability to carefully plan for a beneficial future with imagination and faith.

Judith Paris Roth
Editor-in-Chief
Optical Information Systems
Spring 1990

Introduction

Interactive optical technologies—videodisc, CD-ROM, CD-I, CD-V, and DVI—offer great promise for human learning in all education and training arenas. Already, optical systems courseware programs are viewed by students of all ages in all types of classroom settings—from elementary schools to universities, from corporate suites to factory floors. In fact, at the close of the 1980s, the breadth and variety of the current education/training markets and their respective applications of interactive optical technologies may have hindered the development of a comprehensive description of optical media's overall contribution to education.

Education and training are both large and complex fields with specializations that do not communicate closely with each other, i.e., public education does not typically remain abreast of developments in corporate training methodologies or technologies. Further, the varied and multi-featured attributes of optical media have led to one-at-a-time, one-of-a-kind descriptions of each of the technologies. Individual books or articles have typically concentrated upon only one medium. For example, publications in the early 1980s were chiefly concerned with videodisc. More recently, individual publications have solely addressed CD-ROM or CD-I. The first publication dedicated solely to DVI is yet to appear, but its arrival appears imminent.

It is the purpose of this book to provide the reader with an integrated description of all extant interactive optical technologies. This description concentrates upon the current and projected usage of the technologies in the education and training markets in the United States, Canada, Great Britain, and Europe.

The book is organized into two sections. The first section emphasizes the educational applications of interactive optical media, describes interactive optical technologies, defines the respective training and education markets, and discusses multi-optical design issues. The second section analyzes the trends that will affect future usage of interactive optical media in education and training markets.

The technologies encompassed in this coverage include interactive videodisc, CD-ROM, CD-I, CDV, and DVI. Chapter 2 provides a description of each technology, including its history, manufacturing process, basic working principles, and video/audio/data storage features.

An in-depth examination of optical media's courseware characteristics is contributed by Dr. Jean-pierre Isbouts of Philips/DuPont Optical. In Chapter 11 Dr. Isbouts focuses on the differences between analog and digital media and explains how those differences necessarily affect both the conceptualization and design of the courseware of the two medias.

The education and training markets described in this book were drawn from the 11-market optical media paradigm presented by Rockley Miller, editor and publisher of the *Videodisc Monitor*, at the 1988 SALT Conference (Society for Applied Learning). In his presentation, Miller called training the "bread and butter" of the interactive optical media industry (Miller, 1988). To underscore that remark, he presented figures indicating that training-related expenditures (not including medicine and public education) accounted for 31 percent of the interactive videodisc market in 1988.

This book addresses training, education, and medical markets as per Miller's paradigm. However, for a more thorough examination, training is broken into three submarkets: industrial skills, management/professional, and government.

Five major education and training markets and their respective usage of interactive optical technologies are discussed in the following chapters:

Chapter 3: Industrial Training
Chapter 4: Management and Professional Education
Chapter 5: Medicine and Health Sciences Training
Chapter 6: Public, Higher, and Adult Education
Chapter 7: Government Training

Identifiable characteristics divide these training specializations in many ways: organizational structures, desired learner outcomes, learner characteristics, budgets, acceptance of change, etc.

While divisions are evident, it must be understood that overlap between these markets also occurs. Many optical-based courseware programs serve two markets. For example, videodisc programs designed to build end-user PC skills could theoretically be used in industrial training programs as well as in adult education community-based programs. And at least one videodisc program, developed by Harvard Law School, can serve the needs of three markets. The program can be used for professional training by law firms, for higher education in law schools, and for government training in public defenders' offices.

As referred to herein, primarily in Chapter 3, "industrial training" refers to the development of nonmanagerial, technical, and nontechnical skills in industry. This type of training typically applies to a specific job (precision production, clerical) and is not global in nature. While such training often has its basis in theory, it usually focuses on specific applications and is frequently sequential.

Management and professional training markets are discussed in Chapter 4. Training programs in these markets do not emphasize specificity or sequenced behavior. Rather, they develop a breadth of knowledge in the theoretical constructs of the respective specialties which the trainee is to synthesize and later draw upon when making autonomous decisions in the workplace.

The Medical and Health Sciences Training market provides good examples of both technical and professional/managerial occupations. Nurses, physical therapists, and X-ray technicians require technical skills training. Physicians and dentists are classified as professionals. However, because of the complexity and vastness of the medical education/training market, optical media's usage for training and educational purposes in the health sciences is discussed in Chapter 5.

While Chapter 6 discusses the public, higher, and adult education markets, Chapter 7 looks at the government-funded training market, primarily for government employees.

The markets in these chapters are examined for their acceptance to date of interactive optical media, for their budgetary commitments to the technologies, and for their hardware preferences. Also provided are the distinctive software features prevalent within each market, the courseware development process generally adhered to by each market, and the favored educational philosophy evidenced by each individual market. Because it is not possible to provide descriptions of all available courseware for all markets, examples of courseware most representative for each market are included. Available evaluation data concerning the effectiveness of the media in each particular market are also provided.

The book also describes and provides an analysis of the trends that will affect the future usage of interactive optical media in those same education and training markets in Western society.

1
Educational/Training Capabilities of Interactive Optical Technologies

T he educational potential of interactive optical technologies—with their ability to emulate and stimulate human thinking—far exceeds that of traditional communications media such as print, radio, and television. Even the newer learning media, such as videocassette recordings or computer-based software, are not able to provide a student or trainee with the complex problem-solving simulations afforded by well-designed interactive optical courseware.

However, a word of caution is in order. While these media do offer unparalleled educational benefits, they were often over-represented by early proponents. Videodisc adherents, in particular, were most articulate concerning the educational power of optical-based curricula and at times described the technology in almost "magical" terms. One educator, "who would probably prefer to remain nameless," was heard to predict at a 1975 videodisc conference (without discs and players) that paper, pencils, and perhaps even language would be obsolete when videodisc technology came into common usage (Daynes, 1984). Later, in the early 1980s, Uhlig (1982) argued that videodisc would be one of the five great inventions in the history of mankind that dramatically changed the ability to teach. According to Uhlig, interactive videodisc was to have an impact upon education comparable to speaking, writing, the printing press, and the computer.

This chapter does not attribute any "magical" qualities to optical technologies in education, but does recognize the sound educational potential these media can provide. It is the purpose of this chapter to briefly describe the educational/training applications—both theoretical and practical—of interactive courseware.

And as a second caution to the reader, the description should indeed be considered "brief." Researchers will explore the theoretical issues surrounding these media for years to come and will likely produce volumes of studies. Practical capabilities of the media are already being utilized and will be expanded in usage, and many practical "how-to" manuals will likely be written in the future.

Theoretical Concepts

Future scholars will increase our knowledge of the theoretical underpinnings of optical multimedia that best serve learning and cognition. Three major theoretical concepts that have already received attention are interactivity, simulation capabilities, and development of higher-order thinking skills.

Interactivity

Interactivity is an elusive concept and a term that has been haphazardly applied to most computer-based software. As early as 1983, Cohen complained that "interactive" had become an overworked catch-all phrase that had come to represent many different applications using a computer—not all of those applications being different from traditional linear media and not all being better than well-designed linear media. Too often, the term "interactive" has been used to describe the "stop and go" command/response pattern by which the learner inputs data to a computer and the computer responds electronically.

However, optical courseware can afford interactive construction of messages within the learner's mind. Uhlig (1982) proposed that individuals constantly build a model of the world and constantly measure this model against reality. Optical courseware can be a tool with which learners can make those comparisons—interact with their own mental models, as it were. The courseware can provide a means for learners to go back and forth between the program's content and their own experience, checking the accuracy of their perceptions against verbal and symbolic constructions of these perceptions.

Simulation Capabilities

Properly designed optical curricula, particularly on videodisc and DVI, can provide simulations so authentic that they "feel real." Simulations allow students to experiment with, manipulate, and apply abstract concepts to a situation that approximates reality.

At the 1989 Orlando SALT Conference (Society for Applied Learning), David Lubin of Spectrum compared simulations to the apprenticeship pattern which was the dominant teaching/learning methodology until the late Industrial Age. Until very recently in human history, most learners observed and interacted with master teachers or craftspeople. By observing, practicing, and receiving feedback, the learner was able to become versed in the desired skill. In fact, Lubin speculated that the "learning by doing" or apprenticeship methodology activates some kind of primitive response system in the learner. Simulations, especially those with video, are the closest approximation of the apprenticeship methodology available to modern students.

Development of Higher-Order Thinking Skills

Optical courseware has great potential for the development of higher-order thinking skills. These skills are nonalgorithmic and complex, yield multiple solutions, involve application of multiple criteria, often involve uncertainty, impose meaning, and are self-regulating and effortful (Resnick, 1987). Modern cognitive theory stresses that curricula must be thinking-centered and meaning-centered for the development of these higher order skills. That means a student must elaborate and question, examine new information in relation to other information, and build new knowledge structures (Resnick & Klopfer, 1989).

A learner maneuvering through a multimedia optical program (with extensive text, audio, and video resources) can "make sense" of the topic by constructing ideas, not memorizing information.

Further, the imagery power inherent in optical media is yet another feature which may develop students' thinking abilities. The research is preliminary, but Mary Alice White of Teachers College at Columbia urges that these technologies' imagery capabilities be used to stimulate thinking (White, 1989). She likens imagery to a powerful thinking tool, as it has been known to be for scientists, including Einstein. White wrote that "imagery is the new language of the technologies...and may lead us into problem solving that is more global, more interconnected..."

Theoretical capabilities are essential, but practical capabilities of optical media are equally important to educators and trainers.

Practical Capabilities

Educators and trainers for all ages of students and trainees now have substantial experiential knowledge concerning the practical use of videodisc in classrooms and training centers. Unfortunately, not a great deal has been done to compile this "how-to" information into manuals or guides for use by trainers and educators new to the technology. In one of the first textbooks for practitioners, Martina Lewis' *Videodiscs for English Classes,* the author describes how to use generic videodiscs to teach secondary English. Similar how-to texts (print- or optical-based) will need to be produced for maximum development of the education and training markets.

As for the newer CD-ROM-based technologies, few manuals or texts have been produced for the end-user needing practical applications. As these technologies mature and come into more common usage, manuals will surely be written.

Six powerful and practical characteristics of optical media are covered in the following section and are as follows:

- adaptability
- convenience
- cost effectiveness
- dense data storage
- usefulness as a research tool
- individualized delivery

Adaptability

Due to its adaptability, optical media can provide archives of many types of information that can be instantly and randomly accessed and combined for many different purposes. Teaching Technologies, a full-service firm that markets optical hardware and courseware and consults for schools, universities, and corporate media developers, prepared a list of common uses of optical courseware:

- as an archive
- to control demonstrations
- to illustrate lecture material
- as a dynamic textbook for student study and review
- for desktop publishing
- as a tool for creating videotapes
- to give tests

- for interactive individualized instruction
- for student projects
- to introduce students to programming
(Blodget, 1989)

Convenience

Optical multimedia curricula can provide "education on demand" for individuals or small groups of learners. This "on demand" feature is useful for new employees, but even more so for long-standing employees who want to refresh specific skills or review certain facts. For example, IBM representative Winters (1989) described a videodisc program on inventory management that can be viewed by an IBM salesperson immediately before a sales call. It would not be possible to schedule a class or small lecture group before each sales call for individual salespeople desiring a refresher session. Yet an optical courseware program is available "on demand."

Cost Effectiveness

Particularly with simulations, optical courseware can reduce the cost of many kinds of training. For example, because the use of actual facilities and equipment in health-care institutions is extremely expensive, Rediffusion Simulation, Inc. and the University of California-San Diego explored the use of videodisc-based simulations for training of anesthesiologists whose real-world training experiences in actual operating rooms cost at least $600 an hour.

A second cost-effective benefit of multimedia optical is that it can reduce travel budgets for large firms with numerous locations. Instead of flying employees to traditional training sessions, firms can use videodisc curricula to schedule individual or small-group sessions on location.

Dense Data Storage

Optical media's storage capabilities are especially valuable for education and training programs requiring the use of large databases. CD-ROM is particularly suited for the ever-growing amount of textual information available to technical professions, science, and medicine. Generic archival videodisc programs offer similar storage capabilities for photographs, drawings, graphs, and motion sequences within a given topic area.

Dense data storage capacities also enable designers to build optical programs with numerous skill levels. This characteristic is discussed further in the "Individualized Delivery" section below.

Usefulness as a Research Tool

Interactive optical programs designed to track learners' responses are excellent research tools when programmed to collect data from those responses. Mary Ann Gunderson at USC's Annenberg School of Communications developed an InfoWindow program that not only provides information to cancer patients, but also collects research data by tracking the kinds of information most requested by the patients and their families. Once analyzed, such information will help health-care professionals to understand and address cancer patients' chief areas of concern in future patient-education programs.

Individualized Delivery

With proper design, optical media technologies can deliver the most individualized curriculum available to education and training.

Multi-modality presentations integrating video, audio, text, and graphics into one lesson contrast with traditional education approaches which utilize one, or at best, two media. The sense of touch has even been integrated into innovative programs such as Hon's "Cardiopulmonary Resuscitation (CPR)" videodisc/mannequin configuration. The CPR student must apply appropriate pressure to the mannequin which is wired with burglar-alarm sensors and mercury balances to respond to the physical movements associated with CPR.

But more important, multimedia optical curricula can deliver individualized lessons appropriate to a student's favored learning modality. Visual learners can select or be branched to learning sequences that are presented visually, perhaps with video, still frames, or text. Auditory learners can select or be branched to lesson sequences that deliver the same content in audio—perhaps with oral folktales, music, or chanting.

Individualized delivery via optical media is further strengthened by the courseware's ability to store many multi-level lessons. Dense storage capacities make it possible to store lessons for learners who are literally years apart in their skill levels. For example, the Education Systems Corporation's CD-ROM math series has math lessons for students from kindergarten through eighth grade (see Chapter 6 for additional information on the ESC series).

Interactive optical technologies, with their powerful theoretical and practical capabilities, are already making worthwhile contributions to education and training. Yet, these technologies and their courseware will only become more powerful in the 1990s as the hardware becomes still more sophisticated, and as the theoretical design issues become better defined through research.

2

Interactive Optical Technologies: Videodisc, CD-ROM, CD-I, CVD, CD-XA, and DVI

The interactive optical technology hardware marketplace is dynamic. Announcements are made almost weekly regarding manufacturers' upgrading and enhancing of their systems—whether for videodisc, CD-ROM, CD-I, CD-XA, or DVI.

The term "multimedia"—referring to systems that integrate video, audio, text, and graphics by combining a computer with an optical technology peripheral—has gained popular acceptance in a very short time. In fact, "multimedia" can be found in the headlines of at least one article in every major computer-related journal/magazine in 1989.

The spring of 1989 was marked by statements from hardware and software vendors developing and marketing optically based multimedia products. At Microsoft's Fourth International Conference on CD-ROM, IBM surprised veterans of the CD-ROM industry when it announced that it was getting aggressively involved in Digital Video Interactive (DVI) and that it would co-develop DVI systems with Intel. Along with announcements, actual new product releases—such as Pioneer's LD-V8000 videodisc player which allows viewers to freeze any one of the 108,000 frames on a CLV videodisc—expanded the acceptability of the technology in the educational marketplace.

In other product release announcements, major vendors appeared to be attempting to meet purchasers' cost and compatibility requirements. For example, when Sony introduced its VIW-5000 workstation at the February 1989 SALT Conference, its press release emphasized that the product is a "low-cost delivery system" and also stressed that its new configuration is compatible with most IBM

InfoWindow courseware.

This chapter was written in the midst of one of the richest technological expansions in the optical systems industry. It must be stressed that the information contained herein describes the interactive optical technology systems as they were to be found in mid-1989. With the accelerating rate of change in the technologies, system characteristics such as storage density and price will be upgraded by mid-1990 or 1991. The interactive optical technologies discussed in this book will undergird the "multimedia" revolution of the 1990s.

History

Although optical storage media are often seen by the public as recent, futuristic innovations, the concept behind the media was under consideration as much as 100 years ago. Paul Nipkow, a German inventor, is credited with conceiving of the idea of "videodisc" as early as 1884 (DeBloois, 1984). In fact, Nipkow received a patent for a "videodisc" in 1885. He patented a perforated disc containing a single sperial of holes that were used to record frames of images on a photosensitive element behind the disc with each rotation.

The videodisc concept reappeared in history in 1927 when John Logie Baird, an early pioneer in the development of television in Great Britain, invented his "Phonovision." Baird's device used a needle to read patterns cut on wax album-like discs that could store and retrieve images of objects and people.

Private research continued on different types of "instant replay" magnetic discs or "television discs" through the early 1970s. These developments attracted little commercial attention. Then, in the late 1970s, engineers in both the United States and Holland came up with remarkably similar optical disc developments and playback strategies using lasers.

The Nebraska Videodisc Design/Production Group at the University of Nebraska, Lincoln, was one of the first agencies dedicated to actual videodisc production. The group began in 1978 with a contract from the Corporation for Public Broadcasting, charging the group with "developing the full potential of videodisc technology" (Daynes, 1984).

In 1981 both Pioneer and RCA introduced consumer videodisc players. Three years later, after $540 million in losses, RCA eventually discontinued the manufacture and sale of its capacitance videodisc systems (which used a stylus to physically contact the videodisc)

(Pribble, 1985). The withdrawal of the capacitance system was widely reported by the media—the *Wall Street Journal* called the demise of RCA's system the "biggest consumer-electronics flop of the 1980s" (Landro, 1988). Consumers were not able to discriminate between capacitance and optical laser disc players and often assumed optical laser disc technology was dead also.

However, the optical technologies industry continued research and development and eventually introduced the most successful electronic consumer product of the 1980s—the CD-Audio system.

The CD-ROM format was co-designed by the Netherlands' N.V. Philips and Japan's Sony Corporation in 1979 after three years of intensive research. The first mass-marketed CD-ROM disc was "The Electronic Encyclopedia" and it became available for purchase in January 1986.

Throughout the 1980s, videodisc technology continued to be supported by industrial and educational users as well as by a loyal group of movie afficionados that demanded high-quality video resolution. Growth in the education and training marketplaces was generally steady but not astronomical. However, market expansion based on an increase in consumer-related videodisc players seems imminent as the decade ends. The June 5, 1989 issue of *Newsweek* heralded the "comeback" of the laser player and forecast that new combination systems playing CD-Audio and videodiscs would expand the markets for all optical laser products.

Manufacturing Process

Optical technologies are based on the principle that information can be translated—via a laser beam—into physical impressions on a disc. Those physical impressions can later be read back—also via a laser beam—and decoded into video, text, graphics, and audio.

Information on videodisc is stored in an analog fashion. Each of the 54,000 frames on the disc can be accessed, but the contents of a frame cannot be manipulated. For a complete discussion of analog and digital characteristics, refer to Chapter 11.

During the mastering of videodiscs a laser beam, guided by an FM video/audio wave signal originating from the original videotape, etches microscopic pits into the surface of a thin metal master disc. The master disc is then used in a "pressing" process to duplicate additional discs which are coated with aluminum and sealed with a protective coating.

The playback process for videodisc essentially reverses the production process. After the disc is inserted into a videodisc player, a laser beam shines on the disc's lower surface. When the laser hits between pits, the light is dispersed, but when it hits a pit on the surface, the light is reflected back into a photodiode, which changes light into electricity. The emerging FM wave signal is then separated into the same video/audio signals that were pitted into the original master disc.

Information on other optical media (CD-ROM, CD-I, etc.) is also mastered onto discs by a laser. However, it is done in a digital fashion, or in binary code which is comprised of 0s and 1s. Binary code provides for more usage of raw data by a computer because a computer can process, sort through, and manipulate the digital information. DVI starts with a production videotape much like analog videodisc, but the videotape must be digitized one frame at a time using the scanning and compression facilities of Intel in Princeton, NJ. The process results in a nine-track computer tape with compressed video data that is mastered and replicated onto a standard CD-ROM.

Videodisc

Videodiscs resemble 12-inch phonograph records with rainbow-mirrored surfaces. Videodisc players look very much like VCR cabinets with inner record turntables. As was described earlier, a videodisc player spins a disc, reads the information stored on the disc via a laser, and translates that information back to the viewer in audio and video output.

The Nebraska Videodisc Design/Production Group originated a classification system for the "intelligence levels" of videodisc systems. That classification, which has been widely adopted, is as follows:

- Level 1: The player is controlled by an infrared or wired keypad. The user determines interaction by addressing chapters and frames, scanning forward and reverse, and turning the audio on and off. All branching is under direct control of the user. Sony's LDP-1200 and Pioneer's LD-V2000 are examples of videodisc players that can be used at Level 1.
- Level 2: The videodisc player has a programmable memory. A computer program is encoded on audio channel two of the videodisc and loaded into the player's memory, or the program can be entered with a keypad. Interaction and branching is controlled by the program in the memory of the videodisc player.

Pioneer's LD-V6000A and LD-V8000 can be used at Level 2 (and Levels 1 and 3).

- Level 3: The videodisc player is controlled by an external computer. Authoring software on the computer is frequently used to develop an instructional program and control the videodisc player. Most Level 1 or Level 2 players can be interfaced with an external computer, including those Sony and Pioneer players previously mentioned. Level 3 videodisc configurations range from Apple IIc, IIe, and IIgs computer interfaces to highly sophisticated presentation systems such as IBM's InfoWindow or Sony VIEW Systems (Kurz, 1989).

Features for "Standard Play" CAV (constant angular velocity) laser videodisc format are:

- dual audio tracks
- 30 minutes of linear video on CAV disc
- 54,000 frames held on CAV disc
- each frame can be addressed and presented individually

Features for "Extended Play" CLV (constant linear velocity) laser videodisc format are:

- 60 minutes of linear video on CLV disc
- inability to display specific frames—with the exception of Pioneer's new LDV-8000 player

T.H.E. Report's "Plans to Purchase 1989" survey found that 44 percent of the education market intended to purchase Pioneer videodisc players, while 23 percent indicated they would purchase Sony videodisc players. *T.H.E. Report's* three market segments are 1) schools; 2) colleges and universities; and 3) industry and government training centers. The same survey found that educators planned to purchase 34,000 videodisc players in 1989.

CD-ROM: Compact Disc-Read Only Memory

CD-ROM is used primarily to store large volumes of reference materials or abstracts. Most CD-ROM programs are compilations of already existing databases. A significant exception to the use of CD-ROM for database storage is the Education Systems Corporation's (ESC) K-8 curricular programs (described in Chapter 6).

Use of the CD-ROM disc requires a CD-ROM player hooked up to a computer. The multimedia potential of CD-ROM is determined by the processing power, audio output, and display capabilities of the computer.

Approximately 450 CD-ROM titles were available at the beginning of 1989. The April 1989 *CD Data Report* estimated that an installed base of 1,300+ CD-ROM applications would be available by the end of 1989 (Helgerson, 1989). As for CD-ROM players, the respondents to *T.H.E. Report's* survey indicated that 37,385 CD-ROM players would be sold to the education market in 1989.

CD-ROM's features are as follows:

- stores contents of 1,200 standard 5.25 floppy disks
- stores 5,000 real-life images (as opposed to a floppy disk which can store only five real-life images)
- digitally stores still-frame video images, audio, data, and computer code in any combination
- stores text equivalent to 150,000 pages (about 250 large books)

Sony, Philips, Hitachi and Toshiba, Amdek, and Apple Computer are major firms offering CD-ROM drives. Apple's entry into the CD-ROM marketplace in 1988 was widely welcomed by educational institutions which typically have large numbers of Apple Computers already installed.

CD-I: Compact Disc Interactive

CD-I is scheduled for release to the consumer market in June/July 1990. It will be able to perform many of the same functions as other optical media while offering additional features. It will play music from CD-audio discs and also display text and graphics typically stored on CD-ROM discs. In addition, it will display high-quality video in still and moving pictures, photographs, cartoons, and computer graphics. The user of a CD-I program will be able to search, locate, and manipulate this information by using a control device attached to the system.

Following is a list of CD-I's features:

- stores up to 650Mb

- can handle data from a variety of source media
- natural video still frames (over 7,800)
- over two hours of top-quality sound
- 17 hours of simple narration
- up to 150,000 pages of text and graphics

The CD-I format is supported by Matsushita, Philips, and Sony.

CVD: Compact Video Disc

CVD technology provides full-motion video on CD-sized discs and is a unique method for encoding video, audio, and digital data on the same disc. In interactive mode, a CVD disc carries 10 minutes, or 18,000 frames of high-quality, full-motion video. In linear play, a CVD disc carries 18 minutes of video.

CVD players are available as of late 1989 from SOCS Research, 15951 Los Gatos Blvd., Los Gatos, CA 95032 (408) 356–8313.

CD-XA: CD-ROM Extended Architecture

CD-XA incorporates audio and graphics technology from the CD-I format and serves as a bridge between CD-ROM and CD-I. It provides a variety of functions similar to those found in the CD-I format, but is not dependent on a specific operating system and CPU. This new format will allow publishers to create discs that will be playable not only on any suitably equipped personal computer but also on any CD-I system. This will assist in creating an environment where the CD-I system can be smoothly introduced.

Philips and Sony, in cooperation with Microsoft, are working on joint development of CD-XA.

DVI: Digital Video Interactive

DVI platforms use digital compression and decompression technology—as well as hardware and software products—to bring interactive, full-motion video and audio capabilities to personal computers.

IBM and Intel are currently co-developing DVI multimedia products. Microsoft is also cooperating with IBM to provide open standards and complete hardware and software systems for DVI, including support in IBM's OS/2 Presentation Manager and Windows/386. The April 1989 *CD Data Report* forecast that the personal computer of the 1990s will include DVI as an inherent part of the system.

3
Industrial Training

"The reality of tomorrow's hi-tech workplace has already invaded today's businesses" (Carnevale, et al, 1988).

Today, American industry faces unprecedented training demands in all occupational categories. The work environment has become increasingly complex. A juncture of social, economic, and technological forces has created the need for a work force whose members must possess skills different from those required in the past.

Interactive optical courseware can be a valuable resource in the development of skills required by workers in industry. Technical simulations delivered by appropriately designed optical courseware, particularly videodisc programs, can offer trainees realistic, self-paced learning experiences that could never be presented via traditional lecture or print. CD-based optical courseware, with its unparalleled storage density, can offer trainees individualized and diverse learning paths designed around such criteria as literacy and skill levels, motivation, learning styles, expectations, etc.

As stated earlier, "industrial training" will refer, in this book, to the development of nonmanagerial, technical, and nontechnical skills in industry.

The industrial training market encompasses a variety of occupational categories. This book utilizes the set of occupational categories from *Training* magazine's annual survey of American training: manufacturing, transportation/communications, utilities, wholesale/retail trade, finance/insurance/banking, and business services.

Very often, industrial training is required for licensing or certification. Optical media firms have already moved to develop curricula around such requirements. For example, a 10-disc "Hazard Communication Program" was developed by Interactive Medical Communications (IMC) to meet the ongoing training requirements of the Occupational Safety and Health Administration (OSHA). The IMC program provides comprehensive training on the hazardous effects and the control of specific groups of widely used industrial chemicals.

Market Data

There are indications that interactive optical technologies have not yet been utilized optimally by the majority of American businesses in their efforts to alleviate their ever worsening human capital deficit. In fact, most American businesses are simply not using interactive optical technologies for training purposes.

The latest national figures, compiled in late 1987 in a survey by *Training* magazine, indicated that only 14.7 percent of all U.S. organizations with 50 or more employees used interactive videodisc to deliver job-related training. A *Training* research representative explained that the publication's 1988 survey did not include interactive videodisc because the figures varied so widely that they were considered "not publishable."

There are no figures to indicate how many of America's 1.2 billion corporate training hours were delivered with interactive optical media in 1988. Nor are there agreed-upon figures concerning the expenditures made by corporate America for optical media courseware.

SK&A Research estimated that expenditures for interactive videodisc systems would total $1.3 billion in 1988 and that 80 percent of those systems would be used for training (Emerson, 1988). This conflicts directly with *Training* magazine's survey that indicated U.S. organizations spent $1.87 billion on *all* hardware purchases in 1988 (Lee, 1988).

Geber (1989) wrote that "lots of people in the interactive videodisc industry have noticed some reluctance on the part of training directors to use the technology." Despite that reluctance, industrial training represents a significant market for interactive optical technologies in several senses. In terms of national priorities, optical media can be an important resource in the nation's move to educate productive workers and citizens. In terms of financial returns, producers of optical media hardware and software can move to be included in this nation's training budgets. In 1988 these budgets expended $1.87 billion for hardware, $1.71 billion for custom materials, and $1.23 billion for off-the-shelf materials (Lee, 1988).

Hardware

Incompatibility between videodisc hardware configurations has plagued the industrial training market for almost a decade. Until very recently, potential purchasers had good reason to be cautious when choosing between incompatible systems. Prospective developers were likewise faced with quandaries when determining which microcomputer, which monitor, which videodisc player to choose.

As this book goes to press, the compatibility situation for videodisc hardware is showing improvement. The Interactive Video Industry Association (IVIA) is formulating a set of industry standards (see Chapter 12). Further, industry experts believe that IBM's InfoWindow is becoming the de facto equipment standard for industrial training. "At present, it's the most well-represented standard in the marketplace," says Rockley Miller, editor of the *Videodisc Monitor* and president of the Interactive Video Industry Association (Geber, 1989).

Adding to InfoWindow's dominance, Sony recently introduced a Sony View system that will run courseware developed for the IBM product. Sony is one of the videodisc manufacturers that has traditionally had a strong presence in the industrial training field.

The CD-ROM industry had time to observe the market confusion caused by videodisc hardware incompatibility. The key CD-ROM manufacturers worked together in what Isbouts (p. 101) terms "an unprecedented effort from several competitive computer manufacturers to agree on a common file and directory standard, popularly known as High Sierra." Hence, CD-ROM technology has not been plagued by the same incompatibility issues that thwarted videodisc technology.

However, the advent of optical technologies such as DVI and CD-I has begun to cause a new kind of hesitance on the part of training departments. Danny Hupp, of Pittsburgh-based Partners in Change, regularly addresses training groups on the topic of technology, and he now finds a great deal of "fence-sitting...and waiting to see what happens." Trainers are hesitant to invest in hardware systems. They fear that new and improved technologies will arrive and leave them with obsolete equipment for which no new courseware is being developed.

Courseware Development

Three major patterns of courseware development exist in the industrial training market: 1) the development of generic courseware for large markets with similar needs; 2) the development of specific programs via a contractual arrangement between an optical media firm and an industrial firm; and 3) in-house development conducted by large firms with large training budgets.

Generic

Videodisc programs for large, generic industrial training markets with similar curriculum needs are being produced by major optical media firms around the United States. Applied Learning, located in Illinois, lists various videodisc programs for training large numbers of workers in similar skills. For example, 21 videodisc-based programs for PC end-user training (foundations, operating systems, spreadsheets, word processing) were available from Applied Learning's 1988 "Integrated Curriculum Planner." Contact Applied Learning at 1751 West Diehl Rd., Naperville, IL 60540 (800) 323–0377.

Industrial Training Corporation (ITC) addresses another large, generic industrial training market and develops videodisc courseware to teach the fundamental electrical/electronic skills needed for craft skills training. ITC sells 16 electrical/electronic skills titles including "Ladder Diagrams," "Electrical Control Equipment," "AC Motors," "The Oscilloscope," and "Switchgear."

Contractual

Allen Communication, well-known for its Quest authoring system, has undertaken custom development projects for a variety of industrial training tasks. For example, Allen created an interactive videodisc course to teach Ford electricians how to effectively troubleshoot the Allen-Bradley 8200 Computerized Numerical Controller which controls lathing, routing, milling, and other automated processes used in automobile manufacturing. Allen Communication provides customer support via an electronic bulletin board system and through distribution of its *Promptlines* newsletter. Contact Allen Communication at 140 Lakeside Plaza II, 5225 Wiley Post Way, Salt Lake City, UT 84116 (801) 537–7800.

In-House

Dow Chemical has created its own videodisc training programs at its Texas Operations (Price, 1988). When initiating its in-house development, the Dow team first attended an interactive videodisc training program held by the Nebraska Group. Later, the Dow team worked with the Nebraska Group—a Nebraska scriptwriter worked with a Dow scriptwriter, a Dow producer worked with a Nebraska video producer, etc. Later, when the Dow program was converted to InfoWindow, Dow sent a team to Atlanta and worked with IBM experts.

IBM is another corporation that undertakes extensive in-house development of industrial training videodisc programs. In fact, IBM representative Peter Blakeney (1989) explained that the industrial training category represented one of the primary uses of IBM's in-house videodisc training. IBM does not commercially release most of the programs it develops for in-house training.

Courseware

The following is a description of interactive optical courseware for these industrial training submarkets: manufacturing, finance/insurance/banking, business services, transportation/communications/utilities, and wholesale/retail trade. The majority of the examples are videodisc courseware since that media has the widest use in training. However, one of the first DVI programs is described under the transportation category.

Manufacturing

The automotive industry has the largest number of videodisc players of any occupational category. The June 1989 *Videodisc Monitor* "Market at a Glance" reported that Chrysler had 3,721 videodisc players, Ford had 4,335 players, and General Motors had 10,516.

Ford Motor Company began implementation of the InfoWindow videodisc system for technical training in 1987. Don Robbins of Ford's Technical Training Section explained that InfoWindow's touch screen is especially valuable for the many workers at Ford whose schooling was pre-computers. The touch screen system was programmed to simulate the touch-sensitive control panels of many different machine tools. For more information on this system contact Barbara Schneider of IBM at (404) 238–2731.

Finance/Insurance/Banking

The Chase Manhattan Bank (N.Y.) utilizes an IBM InfoWindow-based program to train some 1,000 new tellers each year. According to banking officials, the new system is proving to be more effective for teller training than traditional instructional methods. It will, they state, eventually replace the current format of classroom lecture with follow-up practice at a simulated teller station. Bank officials hope to cut training time in half—from 20 days under the old system to an anticipated week to 10 days.

Using both presentations and simulations, the modules stress bank procedures, protection issues, and customer-relation skills. The system instructs student tellers in proper responses to various customer requests. Tom Tvrdy, second vice president in Chase's Human Resources Department, explained that "this system enables our tellers to experience as close to real-life situations as possible. It also lets them learn from their mistakes through role-playing observation" (Schneider, 1989). The system also counsels employees on the proper steps to take under stressful conditions and includes a realistic simulation of a bank robbery. Contact Midi, Inc., at (609) 924–4817.

Business Services

Xerox Corporation developed a service training application, "To Bill or Not to Bill," to train new service support staff, service representatives, and billing specialists in handling service decisions. The program was authored with Allen Communication's Quest and runs on IBM-PCs and Xerox 6060 PCSs.

Transportation/Communications/Utilities

Applied Optical Media is developing a "Truck Driver Safety Training" DVI program for DuPont Safety Services, a leading provider of high-technology safety training programs for industry. It will be viewed in a full-size truck cab, in which all driver functions are realistically simulated, with DVI providing views out the front window and the rear-view mirrors.

DVI first decompresses a larger, wide-angle view, selects the portion of the view indicated by the truck's current lane position, and then "skews" this view to keep the distant horizon relatively fixed. Contact Applied Optical Media Corporation in Malvern, PA.

Wholesale/Retail Trade

Learning Systems Sciences, of Woodland Hills, CA, developed an interactive videodisc training program for detectives involved in retail security. The InfoWindow-based program was sponsored and funded by the loss prevention departments of Carter Hawley Hale, Inc., a leading retailer.

The training model instructs retail security personnel on a variety of subjects, including spotting, surveilling, and apprehending shoplifting suspects. Detective trainees are exposed to a wide variety of simulated situations and see the consequences of the various choices they are allowed to make.

Evaluation Data

"A Report on the Evaluation of Interactive Laser Disc System Instruction for Hazard Communication Training at GM" is one of the most comprehensive evaluations of interactive optical courseware conducted in the industrial training field.

The study was commissioned by the UAW-GM Joint Committee to evaluate the effectiveness of interactive videodisc as a training medium. Two hundred workers using safety courseware running on Visage-based interactive videodisc systems were evaluated by an outside specialist for the study.

When the study compared interactive videodisc training to classroom training using videotape, it found that workers using interactive videodisc achieved higher scores. Further, three-fourths of the workers involved in the study preferred the interactive videodisc training method. The study found that interactive videodisc training does not discriminate—it is an effective delivery medium regardless of worker age, sex, years of employment, or years of education. This finding is important in relation to tomorrow's diverse work force. For a copy of the report summary, contact UAW-GM Health and Safety Training Center, 29815 John Rd., Madison Heights, MI 48071 (313) 547-8538.

DeBloois' *Effectiveness of Interactive Videodisc Training* manual reviews six research studies of videodisc programs that are for the development of nonmanagerial, technical, and nontechnical skills in industry settings. The titles of those studies and the years they were released are: Southern Pacific (1983), American Bell, Inc. (1983), Operating Components of Mechanical Systems (1983), Digital Equipment Corporation Studies (1984), Journeyman Mechanics Training (1986), and AEP Power Plant Instruction (1987). Overall, the results from these studies were qualitative in nature. That is, findings indicated that the courseware was "stimulating and motivational," "attitudes were better," or "operators are comfortable using the interactive system."

No evaluative studies of CD-ROM's, CD-I's, or DVI's uses in industrial training were available at the time of this publication. Research is undoubtedly under way or in the works.

This chapter has described the training market's use of interactive optical technologies at the close of the 1980s. Remember that Rockley Miller called training the "bread and butter" of the videodisc industry. With optical courseware's training capabilities, and with the training and education demands of our society, training could well become the "bread and butter" market for all optical multimedia—including CD-ROM- and DVI-based curricula.

4

Management and
Professional Education

"How do we turn John Wayne into Yoda?"
(Carnevale, 1987)

Managerial and professional positions require the use of knowledge that is generative—knowledge that can be used to interpret new situations, to solve problems, to think and reason, and to learn. Regardless of the medium, curricula for managers and professionals must enable the learners to make the transition from *knowing* to knowing *how* to use various concepts, principles, and strategies.

Optical courseware is particularly suited for simulating the complex processes of managerial and professional decision making. In fact, for several years designers of optical courseware for managers have been exploring videodisc-based simulations that will help develop a manager's generative knowledge. For example, Digital Equipment's "Decision Point: A Living Case Study," a prototype gaming simulation for management training, was not designed to supply solutions, but rather to enhance and extend the viewer's judgment (Wyer and Findley, 1985).

Managers and Professionals

Managers are charged with directing the acquisition, allocation, and utilization of human efforts and physical resources in order to accomplish their organization's goals. There are more than five million beginning and middle-level managers in the United States. Additionally, there are two-and-a-half million senior managers who make policy decisions, shoulder overall profit/loss responsibility, and set organizational objectives.

The approaches to management are diverse:

- classical: bureaucratic
- human relations: focusing on the personal adjustment of the individual to the organization
- systems: emphasizing the interaction of activities and people

Interestingly, there are videodisc programs matching at least two of the management approaches. Wilson Learning's "Versatile Organization" is based on the human relations school of management, while Leadership Studies' "Situational Leadership" aligns with the systems approach.

Definitions of the term "professional" vary according to the source. When used herein, "professional" refers to those individuals who utilize principles from the natural or social sciences in their work.

Professionals' jobs most frequently require at least a four-year college degree and often formal schooling beyond the undergraduate level. Technical professionals—who are among the most highly educated and trained of the nation's employees—include 1.5 million engineers, 300,000 computer systems analysts, and 800,000 natural, mathematical, and computer scientists. Typically, optical courseware for professional training should be designed to give learners practice in applying a particular discipline (sociology, computer science, etc.) to situations unique to their line of work.

Market Data

In the 1989 edition of IBM's "InfoWindow Courseware Pocket Guide," 65 videodisc programs were listed under the "Management/Professional" category. This represents an 82-percent increase from the same category's 1988 listing. It should be noted that 16 of the programs listed in 1989 were from Wilson Learning Corporation.

According to IBM's Peter Blakeney, 65 is a relatively small number of videodisc programs for an audience that potentially numbers in the hundreds of thousands. Blakeney also explained that it is difficult to appraise the size of the managerial/professional market, stating there is a large number of InfoWindow systems and "we don't know what they're being used for."

Leadership Studies' "Situational Leadership" program gives an indication of the corporate world's acceptance of management training through videodisc technology. According to Leadership Studies representative Don Brown, the "Situational Leadership" videodisc has had "excellent acceptance" and is now in over 500 installations, with the initial installation in February 1988. Contact Don Brown at Leadership Studies, 230 West Third Ave., Escondido, CA 92025/(619) 741–6595.

Hardware

Managers and professionals operate in a business environment that has traditionally been MS-DOS oriented. That background is reflected in the IBM-compatible hardware configurations being used by these groups for education and training programs.

As in the industrial-training market, InfoWindow has become the de facto standard for videodisc training in this field. Sony's new VIW-5000 VIEW System, which features InfoWindow emulation, adds to the strength of the InfoWindow standard. Visage's upgrade systems enable users to run most courseware developed for IBM's InfoWindow.

Courseware Development

Two courseware-development processes have emerged for the managerial/professional optical courseware marketplace: vendor-sponsored development and internal development of programs for in-house use. In the future, university-sponsored development of programs for professional education may become more prevalent since university staff are well versed in the natural or social science disciplines undergirding professionals' occupations.

Vendor-Sponsored Development

Commercial development of optical courseware for managerial and professional education is being conducted by two types of firms. First, traditional publishers are beginning to fund the production of optical media—videodisc programs in particular—that relate to their established text series. Second, courseware-development firms that specialize in optical media production are also developing programs for these markets.

Allyn and Bacon is a textbook publishing house that "took a

chance on videodisc," according to the firm's representative Sandi Kirshner (1989). The company funded the production of a videodisc entitled "Experiencing Management: What Managers Do" for use in post-secondary business education. Although it can be used as a stand-alone complement to a management-development class, the videodisc was created for use with Allyn and Bacon management texts. Besides marketing the program, Allyn and Bacon also uses it as a promo and gives a copy of the videodisc to each school that uses the company's management texts.

The "Experiencing Management" program contains motion-video segments taken from an American Management Association linear-video program, as well as hundreds of still frames which detail management concepts. The disc is encoded with chapter stops and is suitable for Level I and Level III applications. Contact Sandi Kirshner of Allyn and Bacon at 160 Gould Street, Needham Heights, MA 02194-2310.

Larger firms with in-house training and production departments have the option of producing their own courseware, versus purchasing commercially produced products.

In-House Development

Management or professional development programs created in-house are not always available for viewing by individuals outside the organization. For example, at the 1985 Society for Applied Learning Technology Conference, Virginia Samuelsson of AT&T discussed but did not demonstrate her firm's "Executive Telemarketing Skills Training" videodisc program. AT&T considered the content of that program to be proprietary information and it did not want that made available to competitors.

IBM's videodisc courses for internal training of managers are designed for one-on-one use in the company's Guided Learning Centers. IBM demonstrated a program for first-line managers entitled "The Challenge of Change" at the 1989 SALT Conference in Orlando. This program was designed to teach managers how to manage change and how to build employee excitement about the change. IBM has not made this program commercially available. Contact Peter Blackney at P.O. Box 2150, Atlanta, GA 30055 (404) 238-3139.

Management Development Courseware

Videodisc

Wilson Learning's "Management Skill Development Series/ Interactive" is based on the company's popular social styles programs. The series consists of 10 modularized, Level III videodisc programs with each module having one videodisc and an accompanying workbook. Through the use of computer simulations, games, graphics, computer overlay, live actors, and cartoon characters, the videodisc lessons provide an environment that encourages employees to initiate and direct their energies toward development and growth.

The modules focus on basic skills required of managers, including: organizing and planning, decision making, decisiveness, leadership, and oral communication. The materials are directed toward managers and those aspiring to become managers at all levels. The series is compatible with Sony, IBM, and NCR as well as other MS-DOS-based systems.

Dow Corning of Michigan uses Wilson Learning's "Versatile Organization" program in an innovative scheduling arrangement. The company installed several videodisc systems with these programs at a local university library for employee's evening use. Contact Wilson Learning at 7500 Flying Cloud Dr., Eden Prairie, MN 55344 (612) 944–2880.

CD-ROM

In 1989, no CD-ROM programs specifically designed for use as instructional media for managerial education were available. However, many business-related CD-ROM programs would be useful in management training for teaching trainees procedures for accessing and using information.

CD-ROM databases such as SilverPlatter's "Business Software Database," or CD-ROM-based copies of business publications, such as Information Access Company's "Wall Street Journal," are only two examples of CD-ROM programs that could be used to teach managers electronic data management. Contact SilverPlatter Information, Inc. at 37 Walnut St., Wellesley Hills, MA 02181 (617) 239–0306, or Information Access Company, 11 Davis Dr., Belmont, CA 94002 (800) 227–8431.

Professional Development Courseware

Videodisc

The EmTech Education Corporation's instructional videodiscs on Computer Assisted Engineering (CASE) are the "only products of their kind," according to EmTech representative Richard Kivi. The eight-disc series, which is heuristic in nature, develops the computer software engineers' ability to take concepts and turn them into software programs.

Learners interact with simulations of client interviews and panel discussions, and gain experience in abstracting concepts from the "real world." Further simulations give students practice in the development of computer programs from the concepts abstracted from the interviews and discussions.

The CASE series uses the IBM InfoWindow display, IBM PS/2 model 30 computer, and Sony LDP-1200 videodisc player. Purchasers of the series include American Express, Southern California Edison, Lawrence Livermore Labs, the Los Angeles Department of Water and Power, and IBM.

DVI

The DVI program discussed next is "one-of-a-kind," while the CD-ROM and videodisc programs described are representative of a group too large to cover in these pages.

Ogilvy & Mather, one of the world's largest advertising agencies, is designing and developing a DVI program that could be used within the firm to educate professionals investigating consumer trends, motivation, and the influencing media. The multimedia tool will include text, motion video, audio, animation, mapping, and image processing. It is designed as a compact PC desktop system. Contact Martin Nisenholtz of Ogilvy & Mather at (212) 685-0600.

CD-ROM

As was the case with managerial education, there were no CD-ROM programs specifically designed to be used in the instruction of professionals in 1989. Also similar to the management training situation, numerous CD-ROM programs compiled in the natural and social sciences could be used as curricula in refresher training for professionals or for the upgrading of professional skills.

As was noted earlier, professional occupations require the application of knowledge from specific disciplines. CD-ROM programs, whether abstract or full-text, are excellent sources of the very knowledge required by these occupations. For example, McGraw-Hill's "CD-ROM Science and Technical Reference Set" could be used in training programs for the natural sciences even though it was not designed as classroom learning material. And for social scientists, Silver Platter's "Cross-Cultural CD," with its series of full-text files from the human relations areas, could likewise be used in training programs. Contact McGraw-Hill, Inc. at 1221 Avenue of the Americas, New York, NY 10020 (212) 337–5962.

Evaluation Data

Assessments of interactive optical curricula used in managerial and professional training programs were still largely experiential in 1989. However, one rigorous and controlled research project was conducted by IBM to compare student retention in a lecture-based classroom to retention in three other learning environments: 1) videodisc in the classroom—many students, one instructor; 2) videodisc with groups— five students per station, no instructor; and 3) videodisc with individuals—no instructor.

The videodisc viewed by the student was a Level III designed by IBM to teach new managers how to deal with employees. Results indicated that student scores were higher in the three groups viewing videodisc than in those taught by traditional lecture.

Additional research needs to be conducted concerning interactive optical technology's effectiveness in managerial/professional education. But it is encouraging that IBM's carefully controlled study demonstrated positive results.

Managers and professionals who learn from well-designed multimedia programs now and in the near future will be more likely to ask that their staffs be trained on optical technology systems.

5
Medicine and Health Sciences Training

Medical and health education must respond to a society experiencing rapid demographic and technological change. Demographically, the numbers of elderly and chronically ill patients have increased—as have the specialized training needs for these patients' healthcare providers. At the same time, the rate of change in healthcare technologies and the exponential growth in the amount of medical knowledge have increased the teaching and learning demands in medical education.

Health science education itself is entering a period of change and medical educators have been asked to shift their pedagogical emphasis from a transmittal of factual information to the facilitation of active, independent, problem-solving on the part of the student (Parkhurst & Grauer, 1989). Future developers of optical interactive courseware will likely be designing programs that meet the Association of American Medical Colleges Project Panel on General Professional Education recommendations. These stipulate that medical education do the following:

- promote health and prevent disease
- integrate basic science teaching and clinical education
- develop skills, values, and attitudes to the same extent as the acquisition of knowledge
- train students to be active, independent problem-solvers rather than passive recipients of information (Muller, 1984)

Today's medical education community is almost certainly the most active and best-organized of all the educational markets that are using and investigating optical technologies. It is the purpose of this chapter to provide an overview of the medical science market's many efforts with optical courseware. Because of the breadth of this market, it is not possible to describe all programs or all developments taking place in the United States. Therefore, representative projects or programs are described. The trends that will affect future uses of these technologies for healthcare education are discussed in Chapter 12.

Market Definition

The health sciences field includes health science schools and hospitals, as well as the private and government sectors. The subject areas include all facets of medicine, dentistry, pharmacy, nursing, and the allied health sciences.

As was previously mentioned, the medical and health sciences educational community is perhaps the best organized and most active of all the optical technology educational marketplaces. The market has its own bimonthly journal, the *MedicalDisc Reporter*, published by Stewart Publishing (6471 Merritt Court, Alexandria, Virginia 22312 [703] 354-8155). And the Medical Interactive Video Consortium prints a newsletter that furnishes news about that consortium as well as about other news in the field pertaining to medical interactive video. Contact Center for Interactive Media in Medicine, 4301 Jones Bridge Rd., Bethesda, MD 20814 (301) 295-6263. Information about optical media appears in broad-based medical journals as well. For example, the *Health Sciences Communications Association* (HESCA) newsletter includes Thomas Singarella's "Feedback" column which examines videodisc developments in the health sciences field.

Numerous specialized consortia have been established for health science subspecialties active in research, development, and use of optical media. One such group is Stewart Publishing's MDR Videodisc Consortium (MDRVC), an educational publishing cooperative dedicated to the development and distribution of interactive videodisc courseware in the health sciences. IBM provides support to the Healthcare Interactive Videodisc Consortium, a group of 17 medical and nursing schools in the United States and Canada that are developing interactive videodisc instruction for healthcare training. Contact Paula O'Neill, University of Texas M.D. Anderson Cancer Center (713) 792-6730. Dentistry also has a consortium, the Consortium on Multi-Media and Interactive Technology to Enrich Dentistry (COMMITTED). Contact Eric Spohn, College of Dentistry, Chandler Medical Center, University of Kentucky, Lexington, KY 40536 (606) 233-5995. Veterinary education's CONVINCE (Consortium of North American Veterinary Interactive New Concept Education) is allied with the American Veterinary Medical Association. CONVINCE encourages cooperative development and sharing of interactive video and hypermedia programs for veterinary medical education. Contact Dr. W.F. Keller, President, College of Veterinary Medicine, Michigan State University, East Lansing, MI 48824 (517) 355-7624.

In another area of professional service, the healthcare industry is actively involved in disseminating information at optical media conferences. In fact, Stewart Publishing's annual Interactive Healthcare conference is devoted entirely to videodisc and CD-ROM applications for healthcare. The Society for Applied Learning Technology (SALT) sponsors a concurrent conference for Learning Technology in the Health Care Sciences at its annual Orlando meeting. Regional meetings dedicated to healthcare's use of optical media are also taking place. For example the Chicago Chapter of the International Interactive Communications Society (IICS) sponsored a one-day meeting in March 1989 that focused on the use of interactive video applications in the healthcare industry. At industry-wide optical media conferences, the healthcare group is always well represented on presentation rosters.

Another focus for the medical community is the National Library of Medicine's Learning Center for Interactive Technology in Bethesda, MD. This Center is part of the Lister Hill National Center for Biomedical Communications, the branch of the Library responsible for conducting research in health communications. The Learning Center maintains a collection of courseware for use with microcomputer systems and houses many videodisc and CD-ROM programs. For further information, contact the Director, Learning Center, National Library of Medicine, Bethesda, MD 20894 (301) 496-0508.

The healthcare market's interest and activities are based on its members' recognition of the educational power inherent in optical courseware. The next section describes to what extent the healthcare market is actually using these technologies.

Market Data

Medicine and the health sciences is a potentially large market for optical technology and courseware. A recent editorial in the *IICS Reporter* affirmed this market's promise and explained that "the industry with the greatest growth potential is health care."

Overall, educational services for medicine and the health sciences expend billions of dollars annually in this country. Cassidy (1988) estimated that the nation's hospitals spend $10 billion annually for staff education and training (between $900,000 and $2 million per hospital).

His figures do not include the total for medical training that occurs outside the hospital—which is substantial according to a recent survey in *Training and Development Journal* (Carnevale and Schulz, 1988). That survey found that health professionals rely on schools more than their employers for both qualifying and upgrading training. Cassidy's estimations also do not include patient education, which denotes an ever larger market base for educational optical courseware.

Therefore, educators and commercial firms developing for the health sciences do indeed have a potentially large market. Optical courseware can meet medical training needs inside and outside hospitals, and can certainly serve the education/training needs of medical and nursing schools.

By mid-1989, however, optical courseware was not yet integrated to its fullest potential in the medical and health science market. The use of optical technologies for education in the health sciences by June 1989 was still "fairly low" according to Scott Stewart, editor and publisher of the *MedicalDisc Reporter*. Stewart estimated that only half the medical schools in the United States were using interactive optical courseware. He also indicated that nursing schools were using interactive optical technologies to an even lesser extent than physician preparation programs. Of the 1,200 nursing schools in the nation, only 100 were definitely using interactive optical technologies for training purposes in 1989 (Stewart, 1989).

Thomas Singarella's January/February 1989 "Feedback" column in the *Health Sciences Communications Association* newsletter reported that one in four hospitals plan to implement interactive video systems for specific applications such as physician and nurse education, patient education, consultation, community education, as well as hospital marketing. The survey included 1,200 hospitals of which 460 responded—with 25 percent of the respondents indicating plans to implement interactive video systems.

Health and medicine is currently the second largest market for videodisc programs (Comcowich, 1987). Stewart's 1989 guide to *Videodiscs in Healthcare* lists over 400 videodiscs, but only about one-quarter of those titles are commercially available.

As for CD-ROM, medical education ranked sixth for numbers of CD-ROM-related titles in Bower's 1988 *Optical Publishing Directory*. Eighteen CD-ROM programs were listed under "medicine" in that publication's applications index. Five other applications areas—scientific, general reference, education or social science, business, and computer science or engineering— had more available CD-ROM titles than medicine.

Later figures published in the *CD-ROM End User* (Harney, 1989) estimated that more than 50 CD-ROM titles dealing with medicine or with related topics such as health had been published. That same study stated that the medical CD-ROM market was second in size only to the library market.

Hardware

"InfoWindow claims the major share of the videodisc hardware market in the health sciences in 1989," according to Thomas Singarella at the University of Tennessee, Memphis (1989). Trynda (1989), director of the University of Colorado Medical School's Instructional Computing Laboratory, explained that medical educators may not have favored InfoWindow's interactive capabilities as much as they responded to InfoWindow's provision of a standard and transportable hardware platform. InfoWindow's market share was further strengthened by the Sony VIW-5000 which emulates InfoWindow, and by the Visage upgrade systems which enable users to run most courseware developed for IBM's InfoWindow systems.

Medical educators around the country attribute InfoWindow's dominance to IBM's participation in and contribution to the Healthcare Interactive Videodisc Consortium. Paula O'Neill, the president of the Consortium, also agreed that InfoWindow has provided a "good standard," but added that "the healthcare market is broad enough to support two systems."

O'Neill believes that the use of Macintosh by the healthcare market will not only increase in the future, but that the increase will also "help the overall market." *MedicalDisc Reporter's* editor Scott Stewart also foresees an increase in the use of the Macintosh platform for Level III videodisc programs. However, according to Stewart, InfoWindow will continue to be the standard for commercially produced and distributed programs. The growth in the numbers of Macintosh computers will result from the increasing numbers of professors who will create Hypercard stacks for use in-house to tailor generic videodisc to their individual classrooms.

Courseware Development

Optical courseware for the medical and health sciences fields has been produced by more than 25 different sources including medical manufacturers, medical schools, insurance companies, military medical groups, independent videodisc producers, and pharmaceutical companies. Four major courseware development patterns are described herein: 1) consortium-funded development; 2) university-sponsored development; 3) vendor-based development; and 4) pharmaceutical-based development.

Consortium-Funded Development

The Healthcare Interactive Videodisc Consortium, a group of 17 medical and nursing schools in the United States and Canada, is developing InfoWindow-compatible videodisc instruction for healthcare training. The Consortium's members, who meet twice a year, have established a peer review procedure wherein they review each other's work (ranging from design concepts to review of an actual check disc).

One of the modules produced for the Consortium by M.D. Anderson Cancer Center in Houston is the "Nursing Management of Infection in Immunocompromised Patients." The content relates to material which must be mastered for the Oncology Nursing Certification Exam. The program revolves around an application of the steps nurses follow when presented with a patient: diagnosis, planning, implementation, and evaluation. The learner is placed in an apprenticeship role to the master nurse who models the appropriate nursing process.

During the introduction of the program, students are encouraged to select all answers, not only the correct answers, because it is hoped that the learner will benefit from learning why the answers are incorrect or only partially correct.

University-Sponsored Development

Videodisc programs have been developed by universities around the nation. Many are generic collections such as the well-known "Slice of Life" videodisc developed by the University of Utah to teach medical students basic science and clinical information. Others utilize hypermedia, such as the Case Western Reserve University's program on surgical topics.

A unique use of a university-developed videodisc program is the University of Texas' (UT) coordination of broadband cable and a Level 2 videodisc program on immunology. Students on the Houston campus can phone a UT central videodisc control and tune into one of UT's four closed-circuit TV channels and interact with the videodisc program on the television screen in their location. At a decision point, students punch one of the six correct phone touch numbers as illustrated on their TV screen. Contact Don Macon at University of Texas Television in Houston, Texas (713) 792-5017.

Vendor-Based Development

Medical educators expressed concern regarding the stability and commitment of vendors producing videodisc courseware for education in medicine or the health sciences. "We're waiting for the industry to settle down," commented Thomas Singarella (1989), who explained that the concern originated because a number of vendors for this market have "gone in and out of business."

The series of programs developed by a private vendor that consistently received the most comment from the health educators interviewed for this book was "DxTer" by Intelligent Images in San Diego. These programs train emergency-room physicians via dramas portrayed by professional actors. In one sequence a man enters the emergency room screaming for help and bleeding profusely from a gunshot wound. Attendants lift the wounded man onto a stretcher. Then a nurse looks directly out the screen at the student, and asks "What are we doing to do, Doctor?" The program's creator, Dr. David Allan (San Diego physician and former associate dean of postgraduate medical education at the University of California/San Diego), explained that treating patients in an emergency room is an emotional experience and emotion must be built into each videodisc because emotion keeps the student linked to the patient's problem (Rogers, 1987).

Vendors develop the majority of CD-ROM programs available to medicine. Harney (1989) found that Cambridge Scientific Abstracts and SilverPlatter Information, Inc. dominate the world market for MEDLINE, the largest private-sector database in the world.

Pharmaceutical-Based Development

Pharmaceutical firms have also been active in sponsoring the development of videodisc programs for medical education. Baker Videoactive has produced discs for both Winthrop Pharmaceutical of New York and Smith Kline French and French Laboratories.

The majority of the pharmaceutical firms' programs are used in trade show settings, but several are located at teaching hospitals throughout the country for in-house healthcare training and education. At one point Winthrop installed Sony View systems in an Airstream camper and moved the RV between trade shows and teaching hospitals.

Pharmaceutical-sponsored disc programs vary in content, but include presentations in cardiology, radiology, general medicine, obstetrics, and gynecology. Contact Baker Videoactive, 1501 Walnut Street, Philadelphia, PA 19102 (215) 988-0434.

Regardless of which development process is examined, richly varied courseware as per content, design strategies, hardware platforms, etc., will be found. The next section describes optical media courseware programs in a very broad fashion.

Courseware Descriptions

It is not possible in this publication to provide descriptions of all optically based courseware programs that have been developed for medical and health science education. (Readers who wish to review a complete list of programs should consult the latest edition of the *MedicalDisc Directory* from Stewart Publishing, Inc.) In order to provide a broad understanding of the breadth and variety of development that has taken place, however, examples of programs developed for use in medical school, nursing school, and dental school are provided. Interactive optical programs for medical and dental patients are also briefly described.

Medical School

The University of Tennessee Memphis College of Allied Health Sciences and College of Medicine produced a Level I videodisc with two sections: "An Atlas of Cytopathology" and "The Morphology of Blood and Marrow Cells" for use by health science students, residents, practitioners, and faculty. Each section of the disc has an accompanying syllabus with content outline and descriptive listing of each of 5,457 images. Contact Media Distribution System, Instructional Technology Section, Department of Education, University of Tennessee, 8 South Dunlap, Memphis, TN 38163.

Nursing School

"Intravenous Therapy," a Level III videodisc program developed by FITNE (Fuld Institute for Technology in Nursing Education), is designed to provide undergraduate nursing students with instruction on how to prepare, start, monitor, and discontinue intravenous infusions. The program is divided into six chapters: intravenous solutions, preparing the solution and tubing, starting the IV, regulating the IV, discontinuing the IV, and complications. The program is designed to operate on the FITNE Interactive Video System which consists of an 80286 computer with a 20 MB hard disk with EGA graphics with overlay, but will also play on the IBM InfoWindow System. Contact FITNE, 28 Station Street, Athens, Ohio, 45701.

Dental School

The University of Kentucky School of Dentistry is developing an InfoWindow-compatible videodisc program entitled "Anatomical Features of the Permanent Dentition" with instructional modules that cover surfaces of teeth, divisions of teeth, proximal spaces, and external features of teeth. The program is being designed and planned in cooperation with representatives from five other North American Colleges in the Consortium on Multi-Media and Interactive Technology to Enrich Dentistry (COMMITTED).

Medical Patient Education

"The Story of Maria," an interactive video program designed to teach low-income Hispanic mothers the importance of breast-feeding their babies, was developed by San Diego State University and the Galveston University of Texas Medical Branch. The bilingual program featured audio directions for non-literate users and was developed with Allen Communication's Quest authoring system. The workstation includes an IBM PC-XT, a Pioneer LD-1000 videodisc player, and a Zenith ZVM-135 color monitor. Contact SDSU, Cross Cultural Nursing in Primary Care, 6310 Alvarado Court Road, San Diego, CA 92182.

Dental Patient Education

Videodiscovery developed "Preparing for Jaw Surgery," a Level II videodisc program for dental patient education. Funded under a grant from the National Institute of Dental Research, the program instructs patients on a variety of topics—from types of jaw surgery to post-surgical pain to talking and eating after surgery. The patient chooses a topic, views a segment, and is then quizzed. A printout of the patient's score gives an indication of the patient's understanding of the procedure. Contact Joseph Clark, Videodiscovery, Box 85878, Seattle, WA 98145 (206) 285-5400.

Evaluation Data

As with other education and training markets, the evaluation data from the health sciences regarding the educational efficacy of optical courseware is sparse and from studies with less than rigorous research controls.

DeBloois' 1988 *Effectiveness of Interactive Videodisc Training* manual contains data from only four research studies pertaining to medicine or the health sciences. Two of the studies reported by DeBloois are qualitative and two are quantitative (statistical) in nature. The first study conducted on the 1980 "Work of the Heart" videodisc reported that "students enjoyed the personal control of the materials." The second, "Planning for a Better Diet," reported that 100 percent of learners in an exit interview felt they had increased their nutrition knowledge and enjoyed the instruction.

The U.S. Army Academy of Health Sciences, in assessing the "Paramedical Training" videodisc, found that the group of students who were taught with a teacher-controlled videodisc method completed the training 50 minutes sooner than students taught by an instructor teaching in a traditional fashion. Finally, DeBloois reported that the University of Iowa assessed the videodisc "Pediatric Neuromotor Assessment" and found that the higher scores attained by students watching a videodisc program (versus traditional lecturing) were statistically significant.

Within the next year, research data from a number of evaluation studies regarding the worth of optical media in medical education should be available. Almost all development efforts in mid-1989 include evaluation components.

As was mentioned earlier in the chapter, medicine is probably the most active and best-organized of all education and training markets that are developing, using, and researching optical multimedia. Along with its activity, medical science has provided the optical industry with what are probably the best examples of optically based programs that emulate human thinking and problem-solving. When presenting at the 1989 Orlando SALT Conference, Dr. Joe Henderson (Uniformed Services, University of Health Services) claimed to be "pushing the limits of the technology." His programs (the award winning simulation "Combat Trauma," the educational game show program "Medquiz," and the adventure program "Regimental Surgeon") exemplify the potential of videodisc.

6

Public, Higher, and Adult Education

*"We (technologists) have not even come close yet to making a
difference in the lives and learning experiences
of most Americans."*
(McNeil, 1989)

H istorically, education has been one of the most conservative institutions in our society. In an oft-quoted statement, Admiral Hyman Rickover asserted that "Changing schools is like moving a graveyard."

According to reports released at the close of the 1980s, schools have been slow to adopt and integrate learning technologies of any type. A report from the National School Boards Association (NSBA) entitled "Thinking about Technology in Schools: A 1988 Snapshot" indicated that the process of integrating technology into precollegiate education remained "in its early stages." In fact, the NSBA report specified that policymakers in public schools are especially wary about advanced technologies—and cited videodisc as an example of an advanced technology. As for higher education, its leading general publication, *The Chronicle of Higher Education*, reported in June 1989 that technology's "impact on higher education has been minimal." The *Chronicle* editorialist lamented that higher education's efforts with instructional technology have been expensive, duplicative, and ineffective (McNeil, 1989, p. A44).

Education's traditional reluctance to accept new materials or methodologies is undoubtedly hampering the growth of the public education and higher education optical media marketplaces. With such powerful inhibitors, the efforts of educators and optical media professionals who have strived to develop the potential of multimedia optical courseware in education must be especially applauded. It is the purpose of this chapter to provide an overview of those efforts and thereby give the reader an understanding of the public, higher, and adult education markets for interactive optical technologies.

The scope is broad in nature and descriptions of programs are only a representative sampling of current efforts in these three sizable markets.

Public Education

Market Definition

The term "public education" as used in this book refers to two separate, yet inextricably related institutions: 1) school districts, both elementary and secondary (K-12), that are supported by state and federal funds; and 2) teacher training programs, usually in colleges or schools of education. Technically, teacher education is a higher education function. However, teacher training information is included in this section because teacher education programs are powerfully linked with public school culture and "no technology can be fully effective in the classroom unless teachers receive training" (Office of Technology Assessment, 1988).

Readers interested in the public education market should contact Pioneer Communications and request a copy of its seven-minute "video magazine." The Pioneer-commissioned documentary describes videodisc as seen through the eyes of children, teachers, and administrators. Requests for a free copy of the video documentary must be made on letterhead to: Pioneer Communications of America, Inc., Department EDOC, 600 E. Crescent Avenue, Upper Saddle River, NJ 07458.

Market Data

Maxwell Kurz, president of Ztek—one of the leading firms marketing interactive videodiscs and CD-ROM products to all levels of education—stresses that growth in the educational marketplace has never been steady or exponential. Rather, this market is characterized by surges of growth that are followed by plateaus. Kurz (1989) stressed that the introduction of Hypercard had been the most significant stimulant to growth in the educational marketplace. IBM's more recent introduction of LinkWay is likewise expected to spur growth in education (both LinkWay and Hypercard are software tools designed to help users create multimedia applications).

It is difficult to accurately measure the K-12 videodisc market because many schools and teachers purchase inexpensive consumer videodisc players at local commercial outlets. None of the organizations that maintain tracking data on videodisc players or programs purchased through videodisc industry vendors receive data from commercial outlets.

Industry vendors marketing optical curriculum and hardware to education will share sales data of a general nature. All firms interviewed for this book reported "growth" over the past few years, but no firm released proprietary information such as percentage totals or monetary figures. Videodiscovery in Seattle, which markets about 80 percent of its products to K-12 schools and 20 percent to universities, reported "significant growth" (Bower, 1989). Systems Impact in Washington, D.C. reported that sales were going "extremely well" (Osteen, 1989). Ztek reported "growth," but stated that over the past two to three years the percentage of sales of videodisc players compared to sales of videodisc programs has changed. Player sales haven't increased at the same rate as sales of videodisc or CD-ROM programs.

Courseware Development

The majority of interactive optical courseware and data storage programs for public education are developed by three processes: 1) by vendors; 2) by colleges of education; and 3) by teachers' or districts' "repurposing" existing discs. Vendors and universities typically develop new programs for selected disciplines (science and language being the favored ones). The "repurposing" process is a significant activity in the public education market, but it does not involve new development. Rather, districts or individual teachers interested in videodisc courseware utilize existing Level I programs and "repurpose" those to meet their respective curriculum needs. Each of these development processes are described next.

Vendor-Sponsored Development. Systems Impact, Inc. is the only videodisc publisher to receive the U.S. Department of Education's Program Effectiveness Panel (PEP) award for its provision of courseware that enhances student performance. Systems Impact's "Core Concepts" math and science series are designed for group-based instruction in intermediate school classrooms. Titles of individual modules in the series include "Mastering Fractions," "Mastering Decimals and Percents," "Mastering Ratios," "Understanding Chemistry and Energy," and "Earth Science." Each module contains Level I videodiscs, an instructor's manual, and student response booklets. Systems Impact, Inc. also publishes monthly assessments that report results of ongoing evaluations of its videodisc-based courseware. Contact Beverly Osteen, Systems Impact Inc. 200 Girard Street, Suite 211, Gaithersburg, MD 20877 (800) 822-4636.

College of Education Development. "Critical Incidents in Discipline" was developed at Kent State University under the direction of Alan Evans, director of the Instructional Resources Center in the College of Education. The Apple IIe-based videodisc program features a series of classroom situations that depict student misbehaviors—such as a defiant student refusing to take a test. The viewer of "Critical Incidents" must choose one of five reactions to the simulated conflict and the program presents the likely outcome of each choice, although not every decision is clearly right or wrong. Evans (1987) reported that teacher training for disciplinary incidents is usually in the form of abstract or unrealistic examples from readings or lectures. Conversely, the "Critical Incidents" videodisc gives the teacher trainee a chance to practice decision-making in realistic simulations. Contact Alan Evans, Instructional Resources Center, Kent State University, Kent, Ohio 44242.

Repurposing. "Repurposing" is a process that uses authoring software for the creation of a computer program that accesses a videodisc's audio and visual frames in sequence. Such authoring software usually offers the inclusion of text. By using an authoring system, computer, videodisc player, computer monitor, and a color monitor, a teacher can put lecture notes on the computer monitor and use it like a teleprompter, while having the computer call up the appropriate corresponding audiovisual material from the disc to visually illustrate the lecture points (Blodget, 1987, p. 42). Laserworks is the most commonly used authoring package used in public education.

Courseware Descriptions

Level I "Generic" Videodiscs. Videodiscovery's "Bio-Sci" videodisc was one of the first Level I programs to be widely used in education. (Accompanying Hypercard stacks with a software index are now also available.) The disc contains 6,000 general biology slides and seven minutes of motion clips. A directory is included with the disc. "Bio-Sci" has been used in classrooms at all levels—from elementary to high school to college. Contact Videodiscovery, P.O. Box 87878, Seattle, WA 98145.

Level III Videodisc Programs. The first videodisc program under consideration here is for the Macintosh and the second is for IBM's InfoWindow.

Optical Data Corp., one of the most active firms in the K-12 market, has entered into partnership with ABC News to establish the ABC News Interactive division to develop, publish, and distribute videodiscs for the education market.

The partnership has already produced its first disc entitled "The 88 Vote: Campaign for the White House" which presents primaries and convention clips on one side of the disc and the fall campaign and results on the other. The program can be used as a Level I program or as a Level III program using a Macintosh and a Hypercard stack for easy review of news clips or browsing. Contact Optical Data Corp., 30 Technology Drive, Warren, NJ 07060 (201) 668-0022.

In 1985 the Texas Association of School Boards formed the Texas Learning Technology Group (TLTG) to "bring advanced learning technology to the classroom and to improve student achievement and interest in science and mathematics." That group (funded by 12 districts including Austin, Dallas, Ft. Worth, San Antonio, and Wichita Falls) has since developed a series of Level III InfoWindow physical science courses. The total project will provide 160 hours of instruction and consists of one introductory disc, eight discs in chemistry, and six in physics. Among the instructional programs is a simulated chemistry lab that provides students with hands-on experience. Other programs use math "games" to teach students mathematical principles. The TLTG expanded its pilot test program to school districts in California, Washington, Indiana, and Louisiana in 1988. Contact TLTG, P.O. Box 2947, Austin, Texas 78769 (512) 467-0222.

CD-ROM Curriculum. In what is undoubtedly a cultural incongruity, the most comprehensive and sophisticated CD-ROM curriculum yet developed is being marketed and integrated successfully into the most conservative of all educational subsystems—Grades K-8. Education Systems Corporation (ESC) developed its "Basic Learning System" on CD-ROM to teach reading, writing, and math for Grades K-8. The total package includes the CD-ROM discs, a lab with four to 40 student workstations, and a computerized student management and performance reporting system.

ESC's two new CD-ROM product lines are the "Discovery Learning System" and the "At-Risk Learning System." The "Discovery Learning System" includes Compton's MultiMedia Encyclopedia and the Explorations in Middle School Science series. Articles from Compton's MultiMedia Encyclopedia (which was developed cooperatively with Encyclopedia Britannica, Inc.) are enhanced with sound, video-quality color graphics, and animation. The product, geared to Grades 4 and up, has more than 5,000 entries and 12,000 images. The Middle School Science Program is for grades 6-9 and consists of interactive laboratory simulations, color graphics, animation, and sound. Units and lessons are correlated to basal science textbooks.

The ESC "At-Risk Learning System" is targeted to students most likely to drop out of school and stresses skills relevant to everyday life. The 27 lessons in this series are presented at a Grades 4-6 reading level. Contact Education Systems Corp., San Diego, CA (619) 587-0087.

DVI. The "Palenque" project is a DVI prototype developed by the Center for Children and Technology at Bank Street College of Education in collaboration with the David Sarnoff Research Center in Princeton, N.J. The program is set in the rainforests of central Mexico, was filmed on location, and demonstrates many DVI-unique capabilities: surrogate travel, 360 panoramas under full user control, and a rich audio/video database called the Palenque "museum."

The digitized video, which can be displayed on the computer, is completely in control of the viewer. "It's like you're right inside the frame," explained Kathleen Wilson, the director of the project at Bank Street. The viewer can take a simulated trek through the Palenque site and also access in-depth information about various themes. For example, a student could receive specific information in the form of text, still images, film, and even audio by pressing the appropriate icons.

"Palenque" won the 1987 LaserActive Video Design of the Year Award, and was cited by the Congressional Office of Technology Assessment as a prime example of how technology can be used for learning.

Higher Education

Market Definition

The higher education marketplace includes community colleges, four-year public and private colleges, universities (with undergraduate and graduate programs), and university-based research laboratories.

Higher education is a sizable market that is extremely fragmented. Learning resource centers sponsored by community colleges have quite different purchasing patterns than graduate research programs. The market figures that are available, however, suggest sizable populations as well as substantial budgets. For an indication of population size, there are at least 42 million undergraduate students in the United States today. And for budget size, Nelson (1989) estimated the higher education market niche to be worth $112 billion when she discussed NeXt's entry into the higher education market.

Higher education also had the honor of having a workstation with a magneto-optical storage device designed especially for its market. Steven Jobs' NeXT Computer contains a 256 million character removable, readable and writable optical-magnetic disk that looks like a CD disc. The NeXT Computer is now being made available to the business community, but it was designed to provide a "revolutionary learning and research environment" for higher education in the 1990s (Nelson, 1989).

Courseware Development

As with all markets, higher education has numerous established patterns of courseware development, two of the most common for videodisc curriculum being university-based development and vendor-sponsored development. CD-ROM databases used by higher education are exclusively vendor-produced. Additionally, many videodisc programs for higher education have been developed by "one-of-a-kind" funding packages put together by professors exploring the medium in their respective subject areas. Because of the variety and breadth of the higher education market, it is not possible to discuss all the courseware development paradigms in this book. However, the two most common development procedures are discussed.

University-Based Development. Almost without exception, university-sponsored product development cycles include a rigorous research component. The "Harvard Interactive Video Law" series, developed collaboratively by Harvard Law School faculty and media designers from the Rochester Institute of Technology, has been the focus of research studies examining the effectiveness of videodisc in legal education (Hoelscher, 1988). During development Harvard Graduate School of Education furnished an evaluator to provide feedback to the development team. The evaluation of the series' use by legal experts and its use by students is supported by the Harvard University Assessment Seminar.

The legal series is designed to promote learning by interaction with a hypothetical case, versus learning at the expense of a real client. The videodisc simulations are to be used in conjunction with conventional legal instruction and should extend current law school training to provide a bridge from the classroom to the law office.

By April 1989 700 copies of the "Harvard Interactive Video Law" videodisc series were reported to have been sold to 75 law schools (30 percent of the law school market) by April 1989. Contact HLS, Holmes Hall, Cambridge, MA 02138 (617) 495-1973.

Vendor-Based Development. Scott, Foresman and Company is one of the first major educational publishers to use a development model that combines videodisc production with the firm's traditional textbook operations. SF contracted with Nebraska Interactive Video Inc. to produce the "Psychology Encyclopedia" videodisc to support several of its college-level psychology texts. With this development model, SF explained that it is responding to an increasing demand for video to complement rather than replace textbook instruction.

Two psychology text updates were launched by SF to coincide with the videodisc release in 1988. Teacher's manuals for both texts include instructions for using the videodisc in coordination with the content of the texts. The Level I disc, which contains 14 minutes of motion and hundreds of still frames that define basic psychology terms, can be used by an instructor to illustrate a lecture or by students for further review of content.

Academic research, with its demand for massive databases, is an important component of higher education's overall mission. In response to this demand, vendors have been mastering higher education's common databases onto CD-ROM products. SilverPlatter, which markets a library of CD-ROM products, lists databases with abstracts and journal references for disciplines such as psychology, sociology, and the behavioral sciences.

Vendors have also begun to market CD-ROM local area network (LAN) systems to universities. A 1989 editorial in *CD-ROM End User*, however, cautioned that a LAN—even without CD-ROM drives—can be a potential nightmare and that the hidden costs may exceed the costs of multiple standalone systems that employ multiple CD-ROM hardware and software applications (Harney, 1989).

Courseware Descriptions

The majority of the research and development concerning interactive videodisc courseware in higher education is taking place in two disciplines: science and language. Science's acceptance of optical media for educational purposes can likely be attributed to scientists' familiarity with computers as essential work tools. As for language, higher education has had a well-organized and active group of professors interested in computer-assisted language learning for several years. That group's pioneering efforts are now visible in such associations as the Computer Assisted Language Learning and Instruction Consortium (CALICO), which is very active in encouraging the development of optical curriculum. CALICO publishes a journal, issues monographs, and sponsors summer institutes and an annual symposium where programs and research are shared.

This section will describe representative optical courseware programs that are used in higher education for the sciences and language.

Science. The Annenberg/CPB Project has taken a leadership role in applying new technologies to higher education by committing $150 million over a 15-year period to fund media-based curriculum development. In conjunction with its overall mission, A/CPB provided funding to the Nebraska Videodisc Group/Nebraska ETV Network and the University of Nebraska-Lincoln's School of Life Sciences and Departments of Physics and Chemistry to produce six introductory level science lessons on videodisc. The lessons were designed to explore the videodisc medium and provide technology-based alternatives to the traditional laboratory. In biology, one lesson on respiration and another on biomes were developed. In physics, a lesson on motion and one on lesson energy transformation were produced. And in chemistry, two chemistry lessons were produced that use videodisc graphics as graphics alternatives.

The videodiscs have been made available through Great Plains Network (GPN) as Systems Packages, for demonstration and familiarization use by colleges, universities, and secondary schools with advanced placement programs. Contact Paul Schupbach, GPN, Box 80669, Lincoln, NE 68501.

Language. "Interactions Audio-Visuelles" is a CAV laserdisc designed to present authentic spoken French video scenes to teachers and students of spoken French in a random access and programmable format. The system uses a Macintosh II computer interfaced with a videodisc player and a video monitor. The MacRecorder was used to provide digitized sound and Macintalk software was used for synthesized sound. The program was designed using the Voyager driver and Hypercard.

The disc uses the communicative approach to langauge teaching which emphasizes that language instruction be functional and presented in a natural and informal manner. Contact Alice Slaton, Ph.D., Ventura College, 3875 Telegraph, Ventura, CA 93003 (805) 650-9960.

Language teachers knowledgeable about computer-assisted language learning have been interested for some time in developing computer-interactive audio using CD players in the same manner as computer-interactive videodisc players. Until recently this was nearly impossible because of the lack of adequate interface hardware and software. With the advent of CD-ROM drives that also play CD-Audio discs, however, it has become technologically feasible to develop CD-Audio curriculum.

In fact, exploratory development is already under way. ICD, a publisher of software for language teaching, demonstrated a prototype CD-Audio disc for teaching English as a Second Language at the 1989 CALICO Conference held at the Air Force Academy. ICD's program uses an interactive CD-Audio disc, an Amdek CD-ROM/Audio drive, and software incorporating CD Assist, a CD-ROM access driver. Contact Burl Woodbury, ICD, 750 N. 200 W., Suite 302, Provo UT 84601.

Adult Education

Market Definition

Adult education is continuing education for people who have previously had some type of schooling—even if that schooling was minimal. Adult education students are characterized by maturity, are largely independent in their learning, and are usually employed or seeking employment. With the exception of prison-based programs, adult education is ordinarily undertaken voluntarily.

"Life-long learning" is a phrase used more and more often to describe adult education by the American Association of Adult and Continuing Education (AAACE). Too often, the "adult education" descriptor has been seen as serving only compensatory needs—such as those programs leading to the GED. However, a "life-long learning" orientation is much broader and translates into an educational market for optical media that will reach all Americans several times during the course of their adult lives. Optical courseware for adult education does not have to be limited to remedial reading and math, but can also include topics from the liberal arts, languages, science, technology, and occupational subjects (Holmberg).

Market Data

At the close of the 1980s, optical courseware development for the adult education market was concentrated on the aforementioned compensatory sector of the market. Primarily, vendors were attempting to meet the adult literacy challenge. By 1989 there were 23 million functionally illiterate people in America, fully 10 percent of the population. The dropout rate, a second measure of the state of literacy, stood at nearly 30 percent.

Courseware Development

Development of optical courseware for adult education has been conducted primarily by vendors, both large and small. IBM, for example, has taken a leadership role in the development and distribution of the InfoWindow-based "Principles of the Alphabet Literacy System" (PALS). "Repurposing" development may begin to take place at the local community level with the advent of Hypercard and IBM's Link-Way and the increasing numbers of available videodiscs. With these resources community colleges—which are traditional dispensers of adult education programs—may become involved in courseware development in the future. In at least one instance a community college district (Miami-Dade Community College) is producing adult education courseware.

The programs of IBM and Miami-Dade are described in this section as representative examples of courseware developed by vendors and community-based institutions.

Vendor-Based Development. IBM's "PALS" is an interactive videodisc program designed to teach adolescents and adults with reading and writing ability below the sixth grade. InfoWindow-PALS is based on a fable in which an alphabetic system is invented to prevent war between two kingdoms.

The multi-sensory program is designed to be integrated into a classroom or a laboratory environment and is in use at more than 150 schools, community colleges, and adult education facilities across the country. It is also used in a number of prisons for rehabilitation of inmates, a population with an estimated illiteracy rate as high as 60 percent.

Community College Development. Miami-Dade Community College, recognized in 1985 as the number one community college in America, produces large numbers of educational technology products. Its "Interactive Math: Probability & Statistics" videodisc program is designed for students reviewing general education math, or for those needing to pass a minimal-competency examination in math. The package includes two videodiscs and eight computer disks, a Teacher's Manual, and a student's manual. The program runs on either Apple IIe or Apple IIGS computers. Contact Cynthia Elliott, Miami-Dade Community College, Product Development, 11011 S.W. 104th St., Miami, FL 33176 (305) 347-2158.

Courseware Descriptions

As stated previously, the majority of optical media programs for adult education have been developed to meet adult literacy needs. Therefore, a description of an award-winning compensatory program course designed to teach English-language vocabulary skills—as related to the GED test—is provided first in this section. Second, to illustrate the breadth of adult education, a videodisc program with college-level English text is described. The second program was designed to teach Japanese language skills to fluent English speakers. Both programs seek to develop language skills, the first at an introductory level and the second at an advanced level.

"Earth and Space". Media Learning Systems' InfoWindow-based "Earth & Space" is an instructional videodisc program designed to promote language acquisition. The content is applicable to reading, science, social studies, geography, and vocational guidance settings. Vocabulary and concepts relate directly to GED test subjects.

A Teacher's Guide provides classroom exercises, plus an extensive alphabetical, pictorial, and chronological video index. Contact Media Learning Systems, 120 W. Colorado Blvd., Pasadena, CA 91105.

CALL Project. The Computer Accelerated Language Learning (CALL) Project was established to produce effective Japanese language-learning materials for use by English-speaking adults and college students. The CALL Project is a cooperative effort of Nippon Television Cultural Society and leading Japanese and American educators.

CALL Project's "Understanding Spoken Japanese" videodisc courseware uses television video furnished by Nippon Television Network. The courseware, organized into 30 lesson segments (10 lessons for 1st year of college, 10 intermediate lessons for 2nd year of college, and 10 advanced lessons for 3rd year of college), is designed to be self-instructional and provide the maximum degree of learner control. The learner controls the computer by using a mouse or special Japanese/English keyboard. As of this writing, the CALL Project's hardware platform was being transported from a Japanese SONY system to IBM InfoWindow. Contact Romi Adachi, Kaigai Office, 3505 Voyager Circle, San Diego, CA 92130 (619) 755-0945.

Hardware

The three markets, public, higher, and adult, differ in their computer hardware preferences. The computers purchased by K-12 education will be 56 percent Apple, but higher education will purchase only 29 percent Apple Computers, according to the 1989 *T.H.E. Plans to Purchase* survey. The March 1989 *Electronic Learning* issue discussed public schools' use of multimedia and described the hardware situation as "a heated race between Apple and IBM that shows no sign of letting up." Commodore seems to have reentered the education market as well, and is aiming its efforts at optical multimedia markets with its Amiga system.

While the K-12 market favors Apple Computer configurations, higher education will purchase more IBM computers (36 percent) than any other type. Higher education's preference for IBM may be based in its science and research submarkets whose members utilize MS-DOS based programs.

As per the 1989 *T.H.E. Journal* "Plans to Purchase Survey," 44 percent of all videodisc players purchased by education (both higher and K-12) are Pioneer players. Sony videodisc players are purchased by 23 percent of all educators. And as was also reported earlier in this chapter, public education purchases an unknown number of discount videodisc players from local discount outlets.

Figures available for CD-ROM's acceptance in education indicate that 80 percent of U.S. universities had CD-ROM drives in 1989. The vast majority of CD-ROM products available by 1989 run on an IBM PC/XT/AT or compatible.

As was stressed in the introduction, the overview presented here is brief. Interested readers are urged to investigate further any of the markets and their respective submarkets' use of interactive optical technologies; a great deal of information on multiple topics (hardware, courseware, etc.) is now available. And more information seems forthcoming as interest in optical media seems to be growing daily. McCarthy (1989) wrote that "multimedia (meaning interactive optical technology systems) is taking the educational technology community by storm."

7
Government Training

L ocal, state, and the federal governments together employ hundreds of thousands of persons. All levels of government must provide introductory training/education at some point for these employees. Government agencies must train or educate new employees for their specific occupational tasks or procedures within an agency. Agencies must also provide training courses that are designed to upgrade skills of long-term employees—or assist those employees to respond to technological change. Advanced skills classes are also provided by these various government entities at appropriate times during employees' careers. And safety training is quite often legally required of government agencies.

Multimedia optical courseware is quite often used by other education/training markets to meet the same training needs faced by government agencies. Governments (local and state governments in particular) offer a market with much potential, but with limited development as of 1989. The government training discussed herein does not include the military—an institution long active in optical media development and use. The military's efforts are so vast in scope and so specialized that they deserve separate treatment. Readers interested in military education are referred to separate databases or publications dedicated especially to defense department activities.

Market Data

Market reports on government agencies' use of optical courseware are uneven and scarce. There are a great many programs produced for the private sector (for industrial training or for personal computer users) that could easily be adopted by government agencies. For example, the Los Angeles County Public Defender's Office, certainly a governmental office, has used the "Harvard Interactive Video Law" series originally designed for law school students.

Reports on governments' budgetary committments to the use of optical courseware for training purposes are likewise scarce. Comsell, which will be marketing the "Introduction to Law Enforcement" videodisc program, reported that state and local police departments have not voiced pricing objections to that InfoWindow-based system. Comsell's representative Debbie Kirtland (1989) explained that law enforcement agencies are "not having a problem with the program and their training budgets."

Hardware

All references to videodisc hardware systems used by government agencies were InfoWindow-based. In this sense, government agencies mirror purchase practices of the corporate business community, which has traditionally favored IBM-compatible systems.

No actual record of governmental agencies' use of the other optical technologies (CD-ROM, CD-I, or DVI) for educational purposes were available. Very likely government agencies are using CD-ROM databases, some of which could be used for educational purposes in the future. (For example, the NASA prototype CD-ROM disc which stores data about stars and other objects in space could easily be used for training purposes.)

Courseware Development

Development has been too limited for courseware development processes to have been established in the late 1980s. The smattering of courses that can be found were either transferred from already existing videotape courseware (Florida Corrections Program) or contracted for development (the "Law Enforcement" series).

Courseware Descriptions

One videodisc-based training program for local, state and federal governments are next provided.

Local (City) Government

Police officer trainees throughout the Los Angeles area are receiving training on videodisc courseware entitled "Introduction to Law Enforcement." The course represents 56 hours of traditional classroom time and covers a wide range of subject matter vital to new recruits: introduction to the justice system; professionalism and ethics; an introduction to law training, including search and seizure, use of force, and evidence collection; firearms training and firing range procedures; report writing; and transportation of prisoners.

The videodisc course was developed for the State of California Commission on Police Officer Standards and Training. The package includes eight videodisc sides and runs on the IBM InfoWindow System. "Introduction to Law Enforcement" is being marketed by Comsell, Inc., 500 Tech Parkway, Atlanta, GA 30313 (404) 872-2500.

State Government

Florida Department of Corrections has implemented a statewide program using interactive videodisc to train corrections and probation officers. Seventeen IBM InfoWindow systems were installed by June 1989 in key Florida correctional facilities and Florida Corrections Training Manager David Skipper forecasts that eventually 200-500 InfoWindows will be installed at every major corrections facility in the state.

Corrections subjects in the program include surveillance techniques, stress awareness and resolution, interviews and interrogation, discipline in special confinement, suicide intervention and recognition strategies, crisis intervention, youthful offender programs, and first response to medical emergencies. The video simulations present situations and scenarios that place officers into force situations. The training materials illustrate how wrong choices can affect the behavior of a corrections inmate or probationer.

The video was originally part of a videocassette series but was converted to videodisc by Reflectone Training Systems of Tampa, Florida. The switch from video to videodisc has been positive and has resulted in cost reductions, elimination of wear and tear on the tape shuttle, and a faster search time. Contact Pat Flynn, Box 2150, Atlanta, GA 30055.

Federal Government

The U.S. Postal Service uses videodisc courseware to teach its postal scales maintenance course at the Postal Service Technical Training

Center in Norman, Oklahoma. The Postal Service will be using about 15 to 20 interactive videodisc playback systems to run the courseware for this program.

The videodisc program was compressed from the Postal Service's week-long resident classroom/lab course in postal scales maintenance into interactive video and fit onto a single two-sided videodisc. The disc was mastered using a relatively new compression technique used by the EECO, Inc. firm in Santa Ana, California. Still-frame audio allows an audio signal to be changed into an analog video signal and stored as a still frame on the videodisc. During the conversion process, the audio is compressed by a ratio of 300 to 1. This allows up to 10 seconds of voice-over narration to be jammed into just a single frame on a videodisc. And since there are 54,000 frames per disc, that allows up to 150 hours of audio to be recorded on a single side of a 12- inch disc, as opposed to only 30 minutes of audio per side on a normal disc.

Evaluation Data

Comsell reported that it was evaluating the "Introduction to Law Enforcement" videodisc series in Texas and Florida in mid-1989, but there was no feedback on that program's effectiveness as of that time. With no studies directly pertaining to this market, it can only be surmised that the educational benefits multimedia courseware brings to governments will be similar to the benefits it provides to other groups: increased achievement by learner, more interesting materials, more efficient testing of what learners accomplish, and less clerical work for instructors and trainers (Hiscox, 1981).

Government agencies have special needs for training. They typically operate within a fixed-cost structure and they also often need reports on employee performance standards. Interactive optical courseware is versatile in its application and it can certainly meet the training needs of government agencies—much as it is meeting the training/education needs of other markets. The use was minimal at best in 1989, but with careful attention from optical media developers and government training departments, this market has much room for growth.

8
European Applications

R amsey Malouf of IBM's Euro Coordination Center in Paris
commented that it is "difficult to get a comprehensive idea on
the use of optical technology in education and training in Europe . . .
perhaps because of the 'one time' applications, especially with
videodisc." In April 1989 Pring wrote that "Northern Europe is still
without a comprehensive optical media directory and national market
assessment."

American optical media professionals wishing to stay current
with European market developments on a month-by-month basis are
encouraged to review the monthly "Worldwide" column in the *Videodisc Monitor*. For readers requiring additional information, PLF Communications in London publishes *Interactive Media International*, a
monthly newsletter which discusses the optical media industry both on
the European continent and in England. Contact PLF Communications
Ltd, Towermead Business Centre, High Street, Old Fletton, Peterbo-
rough PE2 DY, UK. All professionals knowledgeable about the European marketplace also stressed that the National Interactive Video Centre
(NIVC) in London—while dedicated to British interactive efforts—is
the best source of overall information for European efforts as well.

Notwithstanding the lack of a single, dedicated European resource base from which to draw, this chapter will provide a broad
overview of European efforts to utilize optical technologies in education and training.

Overview

Optical media developers addressing the European markets face very
different worlds of French, German, Spanish, Italian, or Scandinavian
business. Educational systems also vary from country to country.
Therefore, the use of interactive optical media has developed in different ways from country to country on the European continent.

The use of videodisc in German-speaking countries tends to be for
product information and marketing. The impetus behind German use
of videodisc came from Dialog Video and Telemedia, and was in-

clined toward marketing applications.

Denmark and the Netherlands have several projects in the educational sector, while France has an array of incompatible, purpose-built projects for individual corporate clients (Hoffos, 1988).

The Netherlands national IV center, NIAM, has established expertise in Apple Hypercard multimedia applications, particularly in education.

Denmark and Norway are widely regarded as the Nordic leaders in optical disc technologies (Pring, 1989, p. 46). Denmark's broadcasting corporation, Danmarks Radio, is negotiating agreements with interactive videodisc producers worldwide to encourage the emerging educational market in Denmark by supplementing the country's list of videodisc titles with titles from other countries.

The *Nordic Optical Disc Directory*, developed with the support of the Nordic Council for Scientific Information and Research Libraries, covers optical disc projects in Denmark, Finland, Iceland (where no optical disc projects are recorded), Norway, and Sweden. This publication is available from the Technical Research Centre of Finland (ISBN 951-38-3328-3).

Multinational firms supersede local cultures and use optically based programs that span national European boundaries. For example, IBM's Malouf reported that IBM uses InfoWindow in its European offices for internal training purposes, although InfoWindow is not widely used on the continent for education and training as it is in the United States.

Transportability

Discussion of European markets inevitably raises questions about the transportability of the ever-increasing numbers of American "generic" videodisc programs to the continent. Two transportability issues (technical and cultural) must be addressed if American-produced programs are used by European firms.

Technical transportability concerns arise because American videodiscs are produced under NTSC standards (a 525-line screen, with 30 frames per second). The European video standard is PAL—Phase Alternation/Alternate/Alternating Line—a color standard employing a 625-line screen, with 25 frames per second. A third standard, SECAM, was developed in France and is used in some other countries as well. For most purposes, however, video and interactive videodisc material is made to either PAL or NTSC standards.

Solutions are available for technical transportability. Larger firms produce their videodiscs via more than one standard. For example, Representative Scheuman from United States-based Applied Learning explained that her firm replicates many of its generic industrial discs under the PAL standard specifically for the European market. Hardware solutions to the PALS/NTSC division are also at hand. VideoLogic's Steve Goldman reports a LDP-3600D dual standard PAL/NTSC videodisc player that is used with VideoLogic's DVA-4000 technology.

The "cultural transportability" of American generic programs, such as those programs produced and marketed by Applied Learning or Comsell, is another transportability issue—and a point of disagreement. London-based Signe Hoffos wrote that "American-made management and communication training is too alien for European audiences" (1988, p. 15). However, Applied Learning's Schueman has reported that European purchasers were "very enthusiastic" and indicated that translation was the major problem—not cultural incompatibility between American and various European audiences.

Learning styles and modalities do differ from culture to culture. At some time, the optical media industry will need to address these differences as they can influence the market's acceptance of products. For example, an attempt to introduce American-produced PLATO into a British school was eventually thwarted by the British students who were uncomfortable with PLATO's structure and tight sequencing format which insists upon one correct answer. The British education system encourages creative learning patterns—questioning or exploring—and does not emphasize the one correct answer approach to the extent that the American educational system does. Similar types of dilemmas will likely be faced by optical media firms wishing to market to numerous European educational systems.

Courseware Descriptions

The American and Canadian markets discussed in this book are the industrial, management, medical, public/higher/adult education, and government markets. Examples of European-produced videodisc programs for the industrial, public education, and adult education markets are discussed.

Industrial Training

"Finished by Lunch" is a Norwegian videodisc program designed to teach the use of WordPerfect software. The program uses a dual-screen hardware configuration based on the VideoLogic MIC-2000 controller.

The viewer of the program becomes an imaginary film production assistant who is working on a pre-production crew of a film that portrays the North Sea shipwreck of a Russian submarine. The learner/simulated production assistant is to help the film's chief producer with large amounts of paperwork that must be completed under substantial time pressures.

The viewer is assisted throughout "Finished by Lunch" by a videodisc guide—calm and efficient Anne Mette—who shows the users the commands and functions of WordPerfect.

Kombak, the world's most northern interactive video production company, situated in Kirkenes, by the Russian border, developed the program. For additional information, contact SMG, Bard Krogshus, Lilleakern 2, P.O. Box 301, N-13244 Lysaker Norway, 47/252-0270.

Public Education

In Denmark 15 school systems are testing two videodisc programs designed to provide career guidance for 23 different job types. IVER/I is a program for students interested in careers in computer science and IVER/T is a program for students interested in careers in technology. The programs let students ask questions as if they were in actual interviews. A Commodore Amiga 2000B is used to store the interview responses and a videodisc stores the still video illustrating different aspects of the various careers. For additional information, contact Sven Fredsted, Fiskergade 1, 7100 Vejle, Denmark, 45-583-7111.

Adult Education

Several European nations have videodisc-based compilations that can loosely be grouped under the "adult education" category. These compilations are typically organized to present particular themes from their respective nations' historical or artistic heritage. "Wein Interactiv," a videodisc program that displays the cultural riches of Vienna, won the European award for the Best Heritage Disc in 1987. Italy is sponsoring a massive, three-year cultural heritage project that includes videodisc production of a four-disc production on the art treasures of Florence. Pergamon Publishing of Britain and France's Bibliotheque produced a videodisc archive of 35,000 contemporary images for the bicentenary of the French Revolution. The Dutch Royal Library produced a videodisc containing images of book illuminations and woodcuts.

Hardware

IBM-compatible PCs are the preferred computers on the European continent according to Signe Hoffos (1988). VideoLogic's IVA boards and related MIC system software have set a certain defacto standard in Europe. VideoLogic's representative Steve Goldman explained that the MIC's importance to European markets lies in its ability to address both PAL and NTSC standards. MIC System Software provides backwards compatibility with over 500 videodisc courses produced to date for the MIC system, and offers an IBM InfoWindow emulation mode for InfoWindow courses that have not been converted to the MIC system.

Further supporting VideoLogic's defacto European standard was the contract signed by IBM Germany early in 1989 to market VideoLogic's DVA-4000 technology as part of the new IBM Learning Training System 90 (LTS 90) workstation. The LTS 90 will be used by IBM Germany for both internal and dealer training, and offered for resale to all IBM companies through IBM's Inter-Company Agreement.

Although the use of CD-ROM for legal, medical, and educational databases is still limited in Europe, Italy has a CD-ROM guide to its tax laws and Sweden's PC DATA AB published a catalog of 125 CD-ROM products.

A CD-I based program that examines Latin culture will be developed by the Spanish, Portuguese, Italian, and Latin American governments. The materials will be designed in four languages—Spanish, Italian, Portuguese, and English. The CD-I Project is scheduled to coincide with the Quincentenary of Columbus' landing in America and is entitled 500 Anos Despues (500 Years Later). It will include 10,000 still images, 60 minutes of motion video, 2,400 minutes of audio, and 180 MB of text data. For additional information, contact Carlos Wert, Direccion Educacion y Tecnologia, Serrano 187-189, 28002 Madrid, Spain 34-1/563-9694.

Future

A market survey from London-based Frost and Sullivan, reported in the February 1988 *Videodisc Monitor*, projects the installed base of videodisc players in Europe for 1991. According to that survey Germany will have 26,315 players installed and France will have 37,288 videodisc players by 1991.

The use of optical multimedia in Europe will undoubtedly be affected by the 1992 unification of the European marketplace. The speculation is that the need for optically based training materials that span national boundaries will increase.

9

*Applications in Great Britain**

R oughly speaking, the applications of IV in Britain fall into four
broad categories:

- training
- marketing, including point-of-sale/information, trade shows, and presentations
- education
- museums and exhibitions, archival and resource or reference material

Approximately 65 percent of all IV applications have been in the training area. Point-of-sale and point-of-information applications were slow to establish themselves in the UK, but are now quickly gathering speed. Many of the educational applications have been subsidized by government, while the uses of IV in museums as well as archival applications are only now being explored.

A clear delineation of categories, however, is becoming increasingly difficult, as once-separate disciplines converge to create new forms of communication. Thus, the techniques of information management have informed both the education and training fields. A database can be used not only as a means of information storage—say, a catalogue of parts—but can also form the foundation of a training course or reference material on parts assembly or fault finding. Discs produced for point-of-sale applications can also be used in basic training for sales staff.

Similarly, the "great divide" which has characterized the relation-

---

*This chapter is an excerpt from the Interactive Video Introduction and Handbook, compiled by Claire Bayard White and Signe Hoffos. It was first published in December 1988 from the National Interactive Video Centre, 24 Stephenson Way, London NW 1, 2 HD, U.K.

ship between training and education is being replaced by a more prag-matic approach which recognizes that each of these disciplines has much to learn from the other. There is now a consensus within the training establishment that there is a good deal to be gained by the de-velopment of learning skills, while most educationalists would en-dorse an approach to learning which is grounded in life experience.

Education

A shortage of teachers, a changing curriculum, and financial con-straints are placing pressures on educational establishments which have rarely been so acutely felt as in recent years.

Interactive video certainly has a role to play in meeting these chal-lenges. IV cannot replace teachers, but it can provide them with some resources not otherwise available: for example, science experiments which cannot be performed in the classroom become an exciting reali-ty through interactive video. Most teachers today support a learner-centered approach to teaching; well-designed interactive video pro-vides the facilities which allow students to develop their own learning strategies and make the best use of their individual abilities and tal-ents.

The Interactive Video in Schools Project (IVIS)

The IVIS project began in 1986 with L2m support from the Depart-ment of Trade and Industry (DTI). It was managed until the end of 1987 by the Council for Educational Technology (CET), after which the National Interactive Video Centre took over management of the project, which then became known as the Interactive Video in Educa-tion Project (IVIE). The DTI scheme to put IV systems into every Local Education Authority (LEA) and Initial Teacher Training Establish-ment (ITTE), early in 1988, made IV available to hundreds of schools across the country.

This unique nationwide project spawned the development of eight IV packages across a range of curriculum areas firmly based on existing or developing curricular practice. All of the videodisc packag-es are designed to run on the microcomputers most commonly found in UK schools— the BBC Acorn series and the RML Nimbus.

Practicing teachers have formed an essential part of each of the eight design teams. Teachers, IV production companies, and software programmers together produced the discs to meet three broad aims:

1. To investigate the potential of IV as a teaching and learning resource for schools; to identify its strengths and weaknesses; and to examine responses so that future IV packages are created that meet the immediate needs of both teachers and pupils.
2. To facilitate the development of IV design skills within the educational sector.
3. To explore the practical aspects of implementing technology in schools; to ensure that classroom management experience exists and is shared, and that there is an awareness of the resources required to introduce teachers to new technology.

Field trials are being carried out in over 90 schools to investigate the potential of IV in the classroom. Each school is providing feedback on its experiences and this has provided an invaluable contribution to the Project.

An independent assessment is being carried out by the Center for Applied Research in Education (CARE) based at East Anglia University, Norwich. The results should provide important information on some key issues such as classroom management strategies, modes of use, acceptability of the technology, its effectiveness as a learning tool, and teacher training requirements.

All the packages have been designed to test different approaches to the supply of IV resources to schools. For example, some consist totally of library footage while others have had material shot specifically for the package; some projects permit both teacher and pupil to tailor the material to their particular requirements while others are far more "closed" in their approach. With the more accessible "open" packages it could be said that the computer software will never be "finished" since it is up to the teacher or pupil to create their own routes through the material, selecting sound track and images, moving and still pictures, and directing attention or changing emphasis with overlaid or windowed text. In the case of "open" software, exemplars have been developed which the teacher or pupil can use straightaway, but alter as they see fit, thus allowing them to progress gradually toward the point where they can create their own material. This open software is independent and can be used with any of the packages. The eight discs are as follows:

- Environmental Studies (Moray House College of Education, Edinburgh)

- Siville: French Language (Shropshire LEA)
- Geography (Loughborough University of Technology)
- Design (Leicestershire Centre for Educational Technology)
- Life and Energy: Ecology (Bulmershe College, Reading)
- Missing the Obvious: Primary Education and the Child (Bishop Grosseteste College)
- The School Disco: Maths (Exeter University)
- Challenges: Social and Personal Skills (Northern Ireland Centre for Educational Development and Centre for Learning Resources)

Interactive Video in Industry and Further Education (IVIFE)

Interactive Video in Industry and Further Education (IVIFE) is a three-year program begun in September 1987, with a £1.9M grant from the Dept. of Trade and Industry, to develop IV material for use in industry and further and higher education. IVIFE is managed by the NIVC under Program Manager Malcolm Walton, with curriculum consultancy by the Further Education Unit. All IVIFE projects involve industrial and educational partners. Five are described here.

Interactive Diagnostics: Fault Finding in Advanced Electronics. Interactive Diagnostics is the process used to trace and identify faults in the complex electronic circuitry used in telecommunications.

The disc contains a visual database on the assembly and testing of printed circuitry. Control software facilitates the simulation in graphic detail of diagnostic techniques used on a range of components relating these exercises to the manufacturing processes. This package develops a valuable training application directly related to many manufacturing practices and compatible with the constraints of the shopfloor environment.

The package was compiled by the Northern Ireland Centre for Learning Resources with STC Northern Ireland Ltd and Belfast College of Technology.

PCB—A Board in One! Electronic equipment is an integral part of modern life and the printed circuit board (PCB) is at the center of this technology. Although the production of printed circuits varies among manufacturers, the basic principles are the same and this program provides a comprehensive range of information for those working in the manufacturing, design, or use of PCBs.

The material is presented in a strikingly visual and memorable form through interactive video. It includes a close examination of how components are connected to the boards, whether by holes or surface mounting, and deals with the development of boards from a simple one and two-sided boards to the multi-layer combinations used in electronics today.

The disc and support material were compiled by Crawley College of Technology together with Philips MEL.

The Training Needs of Trainers. Recent research to assess the competence and training needs of a cross section of trainers in industry reveals significant disadvantages in the conventional papers, computer checklists, and guides used to explore particular training needs. Using these systems, trainers had difficulty relating their own skills and activities to those cited and consequently required more guidance from managers experienced in identifying training needs. Such support is not readily available and often non-existent in smaller organizations.

Training through interactive video with support material opens up a broad spectrum of activities and—because the medium is visual, graphic, and stimulating—students can readily relate the images to their own backgrounds. The program can be paced to suit individual needs, enabling the trainer to accomplish a thorough self analysis. When that is achieved, a limited amount of tutor-support becomes effective and cost-effective.

The disc is compiled by Glenrothes and Buckhaven Technical College with Hughes Microelectronics, Distillers Company, and Rosyth Royal Dockyard.

Turning Tools; Their Effective Application on CNC Lathes. This package has been designed to cover parts of several syllabi: BTEC Manufacturing Technology Level N (Objective B2), City and Guilds 205 and 230, EA1 and EA2, apprentice training and industrial training for staff operating the CAD/CAM link.

It will enable the student to plan the manufacture of a simple component, selecting the correct cutting tool to take into account the type of machine, the workpiece material, the quality requirements, and the economics of the manufacturing system.

Students will be able to use the disc in three main ways: either work through the entire video in one session, take breaks at the end of each stage, or use only one part of the package. If students work through the package, they also gain an insight into how to plan the method of manufacture of a turned component.

The project is being compiled by Essex Institute of Higher Education in partnership with Sandvik Coromant UK and Focus Visual Communication.

Effective Teamwork. The key to success for all organizations—commercial, professional, or academic—is productive teamwork. Individual flair is often wasted if not harnessed to team cooperation. The constituents necessary for teamwork are analyzed and explored in this dynamic and visually compelling IV training program.

The program-makers have used proven instructional strategies to deliver a program with high visual impact. It has been devised with the widest range of potential users in mind: team leaders, team members, those within permanent or short-term teams, both in college and commerce—in fact, anyone in or about to enter a team as a leader or a member.

The main aims of the program are to develop members' and leaders' skills and to offer a computerized tool as an expert consultant. The package covers all aspects of teamwork—the individual's role, the organizational requirements for a team approach, and sustaining team momentum. The package is compiled by Slough College of Higher Education in partnership with Royal Mail Parcels and Intra Systems Ltd.

For more information about any aspect of the IVIFE project, please contact Diane Thompson or Malcolm Walton at the NIVC (01-387-2233).

Training

Rarely has so much been demanded from the training sector against a backdrop of skills shortages and financial constraints There is an increasing training need which simply cannot be met by existing resources. IV has proved to be at least a partial solution in meeting the training requirements for a number of organizations. The following sections describe some specific applications of IV in a variety of training areas and industries in Great Britain.

Technical Training

New Skills and Refresher Training. Basic skills training or upgrading is just one area in which IV can play an important part. Some IV programs can effectively simulate actual experience.

British Rail commissioned its first "route learning" disc to help drivers extend their familiarity with the new routes devised for the Thames-Link rail line. British Rail estimates it has reduced learning time by some 60 percent by using IV.

The EETPU (Electrical Electronic Telecommunications and Plumbing Union) is a pioneer in technical training which has always stressed the importance to unions of developing skills and re-training continuously to help their members stay competitive in a rapidly changing world. The EETPU has moved away from "one-off" training in favor of a student-centered approach which focuses on learning for life. To date the EETPU has launched two programs in its projected series of seven interactive training packages on modern electronics. "An Introduction to Digital Electronics" follows the successful "Solid State Electronics," released in 1985.

The Motor Industry—Electronic Manuals—Quality. Many organizations are aware that the conventional maintenance and repair manual can be unwieldy and difficult to use, and that manuals are not always the best way to explain a topic which is essentially visual and practical. Few training manuals contain any diagnostic tools and fewer still are concerned with quality control.

Jaguar Cars has been involved in the use of IV for some time. Early experiments with the technology stemmed from a number of training needs. The increasing use of robotics within its manufacturing facilities created a need to train all employees, old and new. A severe lack of conventional training resources meant that it would probably be more cost effective to produce a basic introduction to robotics via videodisc technology, and IV was introduced.

Then the impact of product liability legislation and the threat of ensuing litigation made the adherence to clear design procedures of critical importance. Jaguar commissioned an IV program on "Failure Modes and Effects Analysis," an analytical technique for anticipating potential failure, its effects and causes in relation to manufacturing design. The program was planned to improve overall design standards and the reliability of the product by preventing substandard products from reaching the customer.

Safety Training

Clearly safety training is an important commitment for many organizations.

Shell UK Exploration and Production wanted to reduce the number of hazardous incidents from the 300 which took workers off the job in 1985. Since 37 percent of all "lost-time" incidents were caused in one way, "Slips, Trips and Falls" seemed a prime subject for an IV program which could take safety training to the workplace, whether inland, on the dock, or in the North Sea.

Produced for the Road Safety Officers National Films Committee, "The Collector" is an interactive road safety program following the movements of four individuals through a variety of road conditions and situations. The "Collector" escorts the casualties from this world to the next and comments on the cause of their death.

British Nuclear Fuels uses IV to train drivers and outside contractors to handle radioactive materials safely. It describes the types of radioactive materials manufactured at the Springfield plant, their storage, and the complex rules, regulations, and emergency procedures required if radioactive material is to be transported safely.

Financial and Business Training

Most organizations need to give new trainees a body of knowledge as soon as possible after they start work. Many of the difficulties surrounding this type of training—staff turnover, pressures of time and cost, individual needs, dispersed groups, and the requirement for some form of two-way dialogue to convey information effectively—are felt by a range of commercial establishments from financial services and banks to High Street retailers.

With more than 470 banks in the City of London, there are major training needs in the financial market, particularly in specialist banking subjects.

Financial i (sic) produced an experimental IV program to deal with one such topic. "An Introduction to Foreign Exchange" aimed to introduce the basic terms and concepts of foreign exchange to trainee bankers, accountants, the business sector, and students of economics and business. The program demonstrated (through a dramatized case study) a number of typical telephone foreign exchange transactions between a company and its bank. Other more recent programs have covered "Eurobonds" and the "Gilt Edged Market," "Interest Rates Swaps," "Currency Swaps and Currency Options."

I.T., Computing, Office Skills

Alfred Marks, a leading recruitment agency, estimates that up to 750,000 jobs are currently unfilled for lack of trained office staff, and that as many as eight million people will need training or retraining in the next decade. Clearly, the automated world of British business is now facing a crisis in the severe shortage of skilled staff and facilities for skills training.

Alfred Marks alone has spent L5 on training more than 45,000 people at its 14 Office Systems Centres, but the skills shortage now demands faster and more efficient methods. To meet this need, Alfred Marks is developing a chain of High Street Learning Centres with a range of generic IV packages from Applied Learning which cover office, computing, information technology (IT), management, and communication skills.

The first two Learning Centres are open seven days and evenings a week, offering conventional and self-paced IV training as a unique opportunity to those who need new skills for a changing job market, whether they be office staff or mothers returning to work.

Of course another large task faces not only those who actually use new technology, but those who introduce and implement new systems within an organization. The key questions relate not only to the components of a system and how to make a purchasing decision, but how to introduce the technology into the workplace. It is the human and organizational factors relating to its use and implementation which often reduce the effectiveness of information technology.

Sales Training, Product Knowledge

Knowing about a project, explaining the benefits of services, and providing customers with the help they need when they need it, are all skills which IV training can help to develop. Many organizations suffer a high turnover of sales staff or of the products they offer. This presents a need for ongoing training which cannot always be met by conventional methods.

Following a study into sales training within the Shell International Petroleum Company, the Supply and Marketing function found that smaller operating companies lacked the resources for adequate training of sales representatives, and wanted more training support from the corporate center although, after slimming down, many areas had no facilities for centralized training. With the high cost of deploying training staff worldwide, and the need to reach as many sales representatives as possible, distance learning offered the only cost-effective solution. Shell had used a variety of distant learning materials in the past, ranging from programmed learning texts to AV packages. However it found that these were too often left "on the shelf." IV, on the other hand, appeared to be a motivating factor in successful training and could be used in a wide variety of work places and locations. Its use could also reduce the costs of travel, accommodation, and absence from the job.

"Selling for Shell" was developed to test the use of IV for sales training. The three-part package covers topics such as the importance of product knowledge, knowing your customer, starting an interview, identifying customer needs, delivering a good presentation, dealing with objectives, and closing the sale. The last part of the course presents a complete sales interview, where the trainee is asked questions and required to make decisions. Another pilot program, "Lubricants," presents product knowledge such as lubricant characteristics, what is required of a lubricant, and additives and their functions.

The response of trainees to both programs has been completely positive. The following features were especially appreciated:

- a logical, structured program using images, sound, and text
- realistic examples
- privacy
- the ability to go at one's own pace

As a result Shell has gone on to develop a number of other programs including a follow-up to "Lubricants" and a safety training package, "Defensive Driving."

Interpersonal Skills: Communications, Customer Care,
Management, Negotiating

The ability to communicate effectively is closely related to sales and product knowledge. In the areas of interpersonal, management, and life skills—commonly defined as "soft skills"—IV has been as successful in imparting knowledge as it has been with the "hard skills" such as mechanical or procedural operations.

Many people learn by trial and error how to deal with difficult situations or communicate with co-workers or customers, and many training methods have been used to improve skills in these areas. Role playing, for example, is one effective means of coming to grips with basic communication skills and handling stressful situations. But conventional training is sometimes impracticable because of time or cost, and good management and communications training particularly requires highly skilled trainers, who are frequently in short supply.

Training in these areas is also often a sensitive issue for those who feel vulnerable in a conventional training situation. Of course IV cannot replace dialogue between people, but it can dramatically illustrate problem areas and present a much wider variety of situations than most role-playing. Perhaps most important, IV is non-judgmental—if we "get it wrong," we don't have to feel too embarrassed. IV can allow trainees to express their thoughts with complete honesty, and explore the consequences of their actions without feeling threatened.

These are some of the benefits noted by organizations including the Post Office Distance Learning Unit, which currently has some 57 IV systems in 19 locations across the country, with plans for 240 workstations across 118 districts.

Many people find their communications with counter clerks at the Post Office more than a little trying, and staff are sometimes perceived as uncaring and even abusive. To combat this, the Post Office National Executive College developed an early pilot program, "Customer Care Counts," which could be integrated into a residential course for new branch managers. The objective of the program was to stimulate discussion in a non-judgmental and lively way, and thus enable new managers to "take away" strategies for improving their own branch's staff/customer relationships.

Following the success of this project, the Post Office went on to develop a generic program, "Leading Your Team." This four-module course is intended for people in their first job as team leader, supervisor, or front-line manager, and covers a range of topics including effective communication, team briefings, one-to-one discussion, disciplinary hearings, personnel problem solving, getting the work done, how to make time to supervise, the benefits of delegating, developing people, induction, coping with change, and motivation.

Two other programs, "How Do You Do?: Making Appraisal Work" and "Learning to Listen," cover areas of Post Office locations and allow managers to "collect evidence" about an individual's performance over a 12-month period using an electronic notepad. This is used to construct a profile according to the Post Office marking scale, and then to complete an appraisal report form on-screen.

The benefits of both programs are far reaching: by improving front-line management skills, the performance of all employees is enhanced. The Post Office has noted that, like any organization, it needs to identify both its strengths and weaknesses—if this can be achieved through the use of IV, the benefits will be passed on to its customers by providing a more efficient service.

Life Skills

Aside from the soft skills required for good communications and management, other, more fundamental life skills are required by a number of different groups including the disabled, those dealing with stress, or those caring professionals who must often cope with sensitive situations.

The Donaldson School for the Deaf has experimented extensively with IV as an effective means of enhancing the dynamic relationship between language and action that is imperative if the hearing-impaired are to communicate effectively. Programs have been developed to improve reading and comprehension and demonstrate the concept of time in relation to tenses, verbs, and the passive voice. In addition, an IV dictionary uses photos and graphics to illustrate the words together with a selection of signs from Signed English.

Perhaps the most difficult task we all face is coping with stress and its related illnesses. But providing individuals with the tools they need to cope with stress has always been notoriously difficult in conventional training. As a viable alternative to face-to-face stress awareness training, the Manpower Services Commission (now the Training Agency) developed a generic IV program, "Stress at Work," which asks workers to contribute their own perception of stress and its causes. Users are then offered the role of stress consultant to consider stress and its causes in the life of a selected character in a fictitious company, Makepeace and Co. Having studied a hypothetical situation, users are then asked to apply what they have learned to themselves and their organization. Users may "participate" in a crisis drama or, via still frames, "visit" the homes of their selected characters and rummage through personal and personnel files.

These last programs all demonstrate IV's facility for providing training which either could not be accomplished at all or could not have been done as effectively through conventional means. The same could be said for many of the program described herein, which bring us that much closer to a real experience. If we accept that we learn best from experience, then IV must have a better chance of success than many other training methods.

10

Canadian Applications*

Most of the work with optical storage media for use in education and training in Canada has focused on the use of the interactive videodisc. In large part, systems have been configured primarily for tutorial instruction, simulation, and testing for a wide range of users and applications but there have also been developments in the area of "point-of-" or "information kiosks." Many of the videodiscs have been produced by universities, government agencies, and firms in Western Canada although a number of large-scale projects have been carried out in the province of Ontario. Not unexpectedly, much of the activity in interactive optical media development has been of a singular nature in that one or two discs were put together as part of a specific project. Instances which reflect a comprehensive implementation strategy are few. To a great extent this has been due to the high costs associated with any optical-based production; however, it may also be due to the fact that both the novelty (lingering?) of the media and, in the case of instructional applications, the lack of demonstrable effectiveness on learning have made those potentially interested in the use of this technology somewhat cautious.

In order to provide a rudimentary breakdown of what has gone on in Canada, this chapter has been divided into two sections. The first will focus on interactive projects which have been completed in the last decade or so while the second section will describe works in progress. Table 1 summarizes projects which have been completed.

Education

Public

In Alberta "Sightlines," a Level II videodisc designed to function as a visual digest or encyclopedia of pictorial learning resources for the

---

* This chapter was written by Tom Jones, Ph.D., Department of Educational Psychology, University of Calgary.

Project name	Medium	Level	Hardware	Target population
1. Sightlines	IVD	II	Apple II	teachers, students
2. Bartlett saga	IVD	III	Macintosh, ICON	grades 7-10
3. Second language teaching	IVD	III	Macintosh	grades 1-7
4. Creative writing	IVD	III	Apple II	language arts teachers
5. Classroom discipline	IVD	II	Sony	pre-service teachers
6. Classroom management	IVD	II	Sony	pre-service teachers
7. Urinary catheterization	IVD	II	Sony	health-care professionals
8. Let your fingers do the walking	IVD	II	Sony	students
9. English for life and work	IVD	I,II,III	Apple II	second language students
10. Michael Petro Ltd.	IVD	II	?	sales/mechanics auto training
11. Surveying technology	IVD	III	IBM	surveying students
12. Anatomy and physiology of the heart	IVD	III	Infowindow	nurses in hospitals
13. Sterile technique at the bedside	IVD	II	Sony	health-care professionals
14. Wheelchair use	IVD	II	Sony	health-care professionals
15. Eco-insights	IVD	II	Sony	general public
16. C.A.S.T.E.	IVD	III	Sony	acoustic sonar operators
17. V.I.M.A.D.	IVD	III	WICAT	turbine engine repair personnel
18. How your heart and circulatory system works	IVD	II	Pioneer	elementary-aged students
19. Canadian Pacific	IVD	III	IBM	secretaries, executives
20. GOLDCOIN	IVD	?	?	trades trainees

Table 1. Completed projects in Canada.

Arts, Sciences and Humanities, was produced by the Ministry of Education in conjunction with the ACCESS Network, an educational telecommunications facility of the Alberta government. The two-sided disc was targeted for the senior high school art curriculum and contains a built-in indexing system and an overview of the layout and material on the discs. Over 26,000 slides were pressed. The content of side one includes material classified as: artworks (world, Canadian, Alberta, student) and themes for study and motivation (earth and earth sciences, flora and fauna, people and the manufactured environment). A section on photographic processes is also included. Side two contains video segments which depict the evolution of image creation—from the oldest images available up to the latest technology.

Genesis, a Calgary-based private organization involved in the study and production of innovative instructional technologies, has produced a Level III system for use by teachers of language arts and creative writing. A series of beginning and ending sequences which depict typical family activities was scripted in such a manner that each combination of sequences would result in a logical scenario. For example, a beginning segment might show a family having breakfast in the dining room. The father might suggest to the rest of the family (mother, son, daughter) that they make a visit to the zoo. Having selected this as a starting point, the teacher can then combine this breakfast sequence with any one of a number of ending sequences (e.g., short action segments at the zoo, an admission into the emergency ward of a hospital, the arrival at the grandparents' home). The task for the student would be to "fill in" the gap between the first and last segments and do so according to the style of writing that was being taught (narrative, expository, etc.). The presentation order of all combinations of sequences would be programmable by the teacher via a "single-key" interface and could be selected according to teaching methodology (group versus individual writing) and the interests of the students.

In the East "The Bartlett Saga," produced by Interactive Image Technologies of Toronto, provides students with an interactive glimpse into the lives of the Bartlett family, a group of United Empire Loyalists who are struggling to survive their first year in Upper Canada. In this case, the goal of the simulation is to enable students with little or no previous knowledge of the era to develop a significant understanding and appreciation of the Canadian pioneer experience. Students must make decisions to guide the course of the story and are asked to make 16 such decisions from a bank of 35, each of which has a marked bearing on the outcome of the Bartlett's survival. To make intelligent choices, students are provided with a selection of relevant supporting research data that can be viewed when required. In this way, good research habits are fostered. By giving students information to make wise decisions and by allowing them to experience the consequences, the simulation encourages students to look at the world from a historically different point of view.

The video segments in "The Bartlett Saga" depict live drama which was filmed on location at an Upper Canada Village in Morrisburg, Ontario, a reconstructed historical site on the St. Lawrence River. The production reflects meticulous attention to detail —e.g., period costumes, utensils for eating, and a custom-built log cabin. The videodisc is accompanied by an extensive teacher's manual that outlines preparatory and extension activities and ways in which to integrate the program into the Ontario curriculum.

In British Columbia Simon Fraser University has developed an interactive videodisc to teach French or English to students in rural schools. The teaching methodology inherent in the disc's design reflects a communicative approach which stresses the functional nature of the language—i.e., asking directions, expressing feelings, and interacting in natural sociolinguistic environments. In terms of content, 12 scenes representing typical urban activities were filmed and the actors were elementary-aged children recruited from a Vancouver school. Animated scenes and supplementary still-frame material were included and the audio tracks contained dialogue for the animated segments. In addition simulated games, quizzes, and other activities serve as resource components. Two instructional approaches are possible: instructor-controlled in which students are directed through a series of activities by a program stored on floppy disk or learner-controlled in which the student chooses his or her learning activities.

In another earlier project, Simon Fraser University carried out a two-phased project to investigate the effectiveness of interactive video on children in grades 5 through 7 with respect to the "heart" section of the curricular Active Health Program. The first phase dealt with the design and development of the disc while the second phase centered on the field testing of the disc to determine the length and type of inservice programs that would be required for teachers and students. The results of the second phase showed that the teachers were enthusiastic about the available technical options—varying speeds, freeze frame, and random-access capability. A variety of audiovisual materials (motion, graphics, still frames, charts, and printer pages) were included to exploit the multidimensional features of the videodisc. The disc was rated as superior to other audiovisual aids, particularly for versatility. The elementary students enjoyed using and learning from the disc and they indicated that the interactive testing was one of their favorite parts of the experiment.

Higher

The Instructional Technology Centre at the University of Alberta has been very active in the production of videodisc-based materials for pre-service teachers. It has attempted to develop simulations which reflect the realities of classroom teaching and provide the undergraduate Education student with an opportunity to address issues which will have to be dealt with in a school setting. The first, "Classroom Discipline: A Simulation Approach," encourages student teachers to begin to think about a personal management style. The students work through individual scenarios that require two or more management decisions to resolve. A second Level II disc, "Classroom Management: A Case Study Approach," presents the pre-service teacher with a situation in which one pupil's problems are studied. In the course of the exercises, the student teacher must make decisions about the involvement of various school resource personnel, parents, and colleagues in order to try and come to some understanding of the diverse factors that affect a pupil's behavior in the classroom.

The GOLDCOIN consortium was a group of seven Ontario colleges of Applied Arts and Technology whose mandate was to investigate the availability of hardware/software configurations which supported interactive videodisc delivery, to acquire appropriate configurations, and to develop and deliver training packages for those occupations designated as critical by the Skills Growth Fund of Employment and Immigration Canada. The projects included (1) micrometer measurement; (2) electronic circuits; (3) trades calculations; and (4) inductance.

Adult

The Alberta Vocational Centre in Calgary has produced, with the assistance of ACCESS, the Alberta Educational Communications Corporation, three Level II laserdiscs in the area of healthcare training: 1) "Urinary Catheterization," 2) "Sterile Techniques at the Bedside," and 3) "Deaf Awareness: Let Your Fingers Do the Talking!" The first focuses on training in the preparation of the patient and tray for the catheterization procedure and in the carrying out of the proper catheterization techniques for male and female patients. The menu-driven videodisc takes the student through the various steps of a successful procedure and encompasses a series of tutorial units, multiple-choice tests, and remedial sequences.

"Sterile Techniques at the Bedside" is also directed toward registered nursing students and provides instruction in the preparation and application of dressings and the maintenance of sterile techniques. A voice-over narrated format is used and the emphasis is on the handling of sterile supplies and the maintenance of a sterile field.

The third disc "Deaf Awareness: Let Your Fingers Do the Talking!" introduces users to the Basic American Sign Language fingerspelling and signs. The goal in this instance is to reduce the communicative barriers that exist between hearing and deaf populations.

Included are both instructional and testing segments which cover the following categories:

- alphabet
- numbers
- word signs including 200 of the most commonly used words which reflect actions, emotions, employment, and people
- common phrases—e.g., "Please, sign slowly," "Excuse me, where is the bathroom?"

Each section is followed by a multiple-choice test. The correct response allows the user to advance to the next question or a new segment. For an incorrect response on the first attempt, the question or sign is repeated in the slow-motion mode. For a second incorrect response, the correct answer is given along with the sign.

ACCESS has also produced "English for Life and Work: Choosing the Right Course," a Level III disc which promotes the skills that will help second-language students who wish to pursue further education or training. Specifically, it teaches linguistic and social strategies for gathering information and making decisions regarding educational and training choices. Students interact in a simulated situation by guiding a main character, Daron, through a maze of personal decisions and educational bureaucracy. The simulation provides English in context and offers new immigrants and others entering or re-entering the educational system a chance to experience reality through the non-threatening medium of interactive video. Computer activities allow users to practice some of the language modelled on the videodisc through spelling and dictation drills. An authoring system permits instructors to create their own drills from a database of words and phrases. The program runs on both Apple and IBM computers.

Training

Industrial

The first and most prolific producer of videodiscs in Canada is Michael Petro Ltd. of Windsor, Ontario. This firm is involved in the continuing production of the training discs for General Motors and American Motors. The General Motors discs were initially prepared for both sales and mechanic training for GM's 10,000 dealerships in the United States. Michael Petro Ltd. has produced completely new discs for the 600 GM dealerships in Canada. Some of these discs have been offered to trade and technical schools to enhance the instruction in such topics as the repair of automobile sound systems, reconditioning, acrylic finish repair, and basic electrical troubleshooting. The discs are all interactive.

ACCESS has produced a Level III system, "Surveying Technology: Using the Rod and Level," to provide instruction and simulated practice in the procedures and skills required to conduct a benchmark and profile level. Users are introduced to the basic principles of using the rod and level and learn how to carry, set up, to take, and to record readings in the field log. The tutorials guide the learner through the procedures for conducting a benchmark and profile level.

Corporate/Professional

In the corporate arena, Interactive Image Technologies Ltd. of Toronto has put together a training system for Canadian Pacific Ltd. in which an inter-office electronic communications system (S2-MR) is simulated in order to instruct personnel (executives, managers, secretaries) in its use. The videodisc program mimics the actual S2-MR system in the context of a tutorial. The program consists of 14 lessons, two practice sessions, and dozens of help screens in a modular format. The program is hosted by an "on-camera" trainer who demonstrates S2-MR's main features. He shows how to sign on to the network, how to interpret the Main Function menu, how to deal with electronic inter-office mail, and how to file and retrieve messages. One big advantage of the videodisc package is that the on-camera host is the only trainer required. After each instructional segment, trainees are automatically tested on their command of the material to that point. Participants go over each lesson until they are satisfied that the material has been mastered. They may also request "help" at any point by keying in a command taught early in the program.

Medical

The IBM/B.C.I.T. (British Columbia Institute of Technology) Interactive Videodisc Development project has produced a Level III disc entitled "The Anatomy and Physiology of the Heart" which was designed to support regular classroom instruction by providing instructors instant access to hundreds of specimens, video segments of surgery and autopsy, medical images, animations, and explanations which could be projected in a classroom. The videodisc program contains a test-item bank and an extensive series of computer-assisted tutorials. Thus, students might use the system to reinforce ideas encountered in the classroom lectures, to explore topics in detail, or to review before final examinations. The estimated total time of presentation for 25 modules is eight hours. The response to this disc has been excellent.

With respect to the structure or instructional design of the disc, each of the 25 topics (e.g., surgical procedures, magnetic resonance imaging, ultrasound) is presented by means of five modes or venues:

1. Overview: these video clips introduce the topic and indicate its relevance and scope. They serve as advanced organizers.
2. Presentation: these segments cover the actual material to be learned. Interaction occurs via the Infowindow touchscreen approximately every 20 seconds. Relevant animation sequences, computer simulations, and still images with graphic overlays are used.
3. Exploration: while the presentation deals with the "need to know" material, the exploration option deals with the "nice to know" information and provides additional examples or views of medical imaging to supplement the topic.
4. Summary: a precis in one or two pages of the key points contained in the presentation. Students particularly like the summary when preparing for examinations.
5. Test: while review questions are given throughout the presentation, this section provides access to an extensive test-item bank dealing with the topics. Because questions are drawn at random and the distractors appear in scrambled order, a wide variety of multiple-choice, labelling, or matching questions may be presented.

To ensure instructional effectiveness, the videodisc program was developed using an instructional systems model. The content area was divided into six major themes and these themes into content blocks. The objectives for each block were specified and then analyzed into enabling objectives and the matching content information. As several different student groups were to use the program, the content was mapped against the knowledge needs of each technology and a control matrix was created to guide students through the interactive program. Extensive subject-matter expert input and formative evaluation with students were used to revise the scripts and the final computer presentation.

In 1982 the Banff Centre for Continuing Education produced a 20-minute videodisc that provides training in the use of a wheelchair for people with left hemiplegia (paralysis). It can be used by patients or those who work with them and has been distributed to hospitals and university nursing facilities.

Government/Military

"Eco-Insights: Ecology of the Kananaskis Region," produced by AC-CESS Network, is a Level II videodisc which introduces users to some of the basic principles of ecology in the Kananaskis region of the Canadian Rocky Mountains. Users learn about the diversity of life in the mountain regions, the effect of winter on living things, and the forces of change that affect the landscape. Although designed as a "point of information" system, a second program allows for general viewing of the information on the videodisc. The content consists of a number of short video segments in three major areas:

- low mountain passes
- mountain winters and living things
- forces of change affecting the landscape

Each segment is accessed through a menu and the menus are organized in a tree structure which allows users to step through topic-related information until the desired segment has been viewed.

Future Applications

Higher Education

The Instructional Technology Centre at the University of Alberta has four laserdisc projects planned for production. Two of the applications will be used as components in the University's Education courses at both the undergraduate and graduate levels. The first, "Questioning Strategies," a collaboration with the Edmonton Public School Board, will provide students with an opportunity to analyze productive approaches to the asking of questions in a classroom setting. The second, "Project Decide," allows elementary school principals to prioritize items or concerns which surface as in-basket items. The two remaining projects will deal with human development and a visual database ("Canadian Schooling Project").

Project name	Medium	Level	Hardware	Target population
1. American sign language in Canada	IVD	I, III	Sony, IBM	general public, children
2.Bow Valley Information system	IVD	III	Sony, touchscreen	park visitors
3. Canadian sign language	IVD	I,III	Sony	general public
4. Forest Fire Control	IVD	III	IBM	forestry workers
5. Questioning strategies	IVD	II	Sony	pre-service teachers
6. Project Decide principals	IVD	III	Infowindow	elementary-school
7. Human Development	IVD	III	Infowindow	post-degree B.Ed. students
8. Canadian Schooling project	IVD	?	?	?
9. Cardiac pacemakers	IVD	III	Infowindow	nurses

Table 2. Future projects in Canada.

Adult Education

The Forest Technology School in Hinton, Alberta, is planning to produce a fire control simulator which will engage learners in the identification of wildland fire behavior, the deployment and effect of resources selected to control the fire, and the choosing of key role players (dispatchers, towermen, pilots) as required. A computer-generated three-dimensional fire growth model will be integrated into the course and this will enable students to observe fire progress in graphic form, to vary fuel, weather and topography types, and to observe results. The six-hour course is divided into three units, the first of which reviews the fire triangle and then tutors the learner in the prediction of fire growth. Unit 2 presents both ground and air attack approaches to suppression and then takes the learner through several steps in conducting a fire assessment. Unit 3, a key feature of the course, will allow the learner to apply acquired knowledge to conduct an assessment and to direct resources through the use of an interactive simulation in several wildfire environments.

Medicine

In addition to the work described above, B.I.C.T. is in the process of producing a second Level III videodisc for the health field. "Cardiac Pacemakers" will be designed primarily for nurses who are enrolled in the Advanced Diploma in Critical Care Nursing and for nurses who require on-the-job training about cardiac pacemakers. Four related topics will be covered:

1. Indications for pacemaker treatment: after reviewing how the normal heart's cardiac conduction system triggers contraction and produces an ECG, the program looks at how a pacemaker can compensate for problems in conduction (heart blocks) and problems in pulse initiation.
2. Pacemaker function: this section shows how the pacemaker senses the electrical activity of the heart and in response to pre-selected indications, stimulates the heart tissue directly. Basic electrical concepts of completed circuits, strength of pulse, and pulse width are identified and illustrated.
3. ECG rhythm strip analysis: this skill allows the nurse to verify the operation of the pacemaker. After showing a simple algo-rithm for a troubleshooting procedure, the system will make a number of problems available for practice.
4. The pacemaker patient: the chronology of events in a typical pacemaker case is followed. Scenes of surgical implantation, discussion of the risk of infection, and psychological concerns are addressed.

Government

In a production similar to the "Eco-Insights" disc described above, ACCESS Alberta is working on a videodisc-based information system for Bow Valley Provincial Park, a popular tourist area in the Rocky Mountains. The system, which employs a touchscreen for input, will provide visitors with information about park facilities and interpretive information about local plants, animals, and the environment.

The Educational Technology Centre of ACCESS Alberta plans to produce a visual database of still and motion pictures depicting vari-ous tourism destinations in Alberta and a selection of motion seg-ments which show activities of interest to tourists. In addition to the videodisc, 10 computer-assisted modules will be developed to access the database.

Summary

The descriptions above of both completed and planned projects dem-onstrate that a great deal of activity vis-a-vis the use of optical storage media has taken place and is being planned in Canada. Primarily, the projects have been in the areas of information stations and training. Looking closely at the work that has been done over the last 10 years, one point which stands out is that the majority of these implementations have been of a "one-shot" nature and that there has not emerged a major player in the area of optical media in training and education, although a number of firms and agencies have vied for the position. It appears as if this will continue to be the case for the short term.

One particular problem for the interested parties in Canada has been the matter of long-term funding. In many instances seed or start-up money has been provided by a provincial or federal department with the intention of having the private sector either follow up on the initiative or, at the very least, recognize the potential of the media. Unfortunately, this has not occurred.

From the instructional point of view, the introduction of individualized training systems has always (with or without the use of optical storage) caused some consternation in the ranks of those who either support or have a vested interest in traditional modes of delivery (e.g., classroom teaching). Nothing has changed as a result of the availability of laser-based workstations. To a large extent, these individualized stations are viewed as a "wedge" in the instructional program and, rather than act as a panacea for the trainers' problems, bring with them a whole new set of concerns (e.g., early completion of material by a student, coordination of equipment). The merging of traditional instructional models with those which result from the introduction of "single-user" technology has proven to be a difficult obstacle to overcome. On a similar note, the incorporation of individualized training systems usually calls for the acquisition of additional equipment and facilities which results in added expense.

So there is much activity in Canada with respect to the use of optical storage media in education and training. Many talented individuals and agencies have recognized the potential for these technologies and have taken advantage of opportunities to put their ideas to work. Undoubtedly, the best is yet to come.

11

Designing for Interactive Media: Analog vs. Digital Domains*

T o date, the most predominant optical medium for interactive programming, used mostly for instructional, tutorial, or merchandising purposes, is the family of optical analog carriers, based on the Laservision technology developed by Philips and MCA/DiscoVision and standardized as the "videodisc." For the purposes of our discussion, we should also include the more recent version of the videodisc developed for consumer markets with a CD-quality, digital audio track. This type is appearing in three sizes: a 12" laserdisc (for movies), an 8" "EP" format disc (for concert tracks), and a small 5" "CD-Video" format (for music video clips containing five minutes of video and an additional 20 minutes of audio-only tracks). In Europe all three formats are designated as "CD-Video" and all sizes are gold-colored to distinguish them from Laservision discs. Due to differences in bandwidth, digital-track laserdiscs cannot be played on European laservision players, whereas in the U.S. most laserdiscs are additionally equipped with an analog sound track for playback on older videodisc players.

However, our focus is on the design of programming for interactive applications, and the key characteristic of videodisc design is that it employs a standard broadcast television signal to create the primary audiovisual material. "Footage" is, quite simply, made by pointing a video camera at a subject and running the tape. In other words: the acquisition of image, sound, and synchronized motion is all handled by video technology. Thus, the problem of videodisc design is how to

---

* *This chapter was contributed by Jean-pierre Isbouts, Ph.D., Philips and Dupont Optical.*

organize a set of video clips in an interactive program that will allow the user to absorb information uniquely geared to his interest, learning pace, or academic level. Videodisc design, in short, is the art of organizing a series of video chapters in as economical a manner as possible while still affording viewers the greatest possible freedom of individual use.

Hence the emphasis in videodisc design lies on a term raised to almost sublime levels in the videodisc industry: "authoring." Authoring is the activity by which instructional designers arrange snippets of video information (usually handed down to them by their customers in the form of training films, product trailers, or collateral data) with such dexterity that each viewer can chart his path through the program and call it rightfully his own. If this sounds like authoring is a task rather separate from the original video production, you're right. In fact, one follows the other in the design process. For purely technical reasons, actual "authoring" can begin only when the production process is finished and has yielded a disc.

Of course, both video production and interactive authoring have a common offspring: the script. Because of the complex charting that occurs in the world of video (not all of it warranted by the needs of the intended audience), the instrument of choice in preparing the script is the flow-chart. This manuscript, which plots the way in which the future viewer can choose his course through the program, is the key blueprint for the ultimate videodisc and is referred to constantly by designer, producer, and author/programmer.

Why this preoccupation with charting a program labyrinth? The answer is simple: because the medium is analog, and because each audiovisual sequence is an immobile, pre-edited chunk whose access, but not its contents, can be manipulated by interactive use.

This is the essential difference between videodisc and "multimedia" digital design: an author/designer has a finite number of ways to relate one video sequence (or still) to another, namely, by placing its playback in a certain predetermined order with other segments. Once this sequence is programmed into the software that controls the videodisc, it is immutable.

Digital Authoring

The digital world, on the other hand, knows no such boundaries to relationships between sequences. Indeed, for the computer, an audiovisual sequence is not a preacquired, single video program but is actually a loosely arranged collage of "files"—data file, image file, sound file, and sequencing file, by which aduiovisual segments can be created, altered, and broken up at will. This has led to a radically different school of interactive design, and one which is summed up in the term "hypertext." Hypertext is not so much an authoring tool but rather an authoring principle—a state of mind. It proposes that a group of audiovisual tutorials should not be pre-arranged as a cohesive program as this limits the interactive intervention by the user to one of choice and pace. Rather it should have an extended network of references, distributed at random through the core "file," usually a body of text. Depending on his mood, his interest or his pace, the viewer can start wherever he pleases, and touch upon "extended files": a graphic, sound sample or AV clip—only if his reading at that time demands it. Access to these extended files is usually offered through pop-up menus or "hot keys" (highlighted words in the core text).

To develop a hierarchical learning sequence for such myriad reference possibilities would be nearly impossible. In point of fact, it would subjectively limit the individual learning experience of a hypertext environment. Therefore, a hypertext designer must abandon the concept of a systematically crafted "tutorial session," with a discrete start and end, and surrender the student/viewer to a learning experience which, dependent on his willingness to explore the three-dimensional AV information at a given time, may yield uneven results .

Hypertext, of course, was first made possible on a wide scale by the Macintosh Hypercard program, which wasn't so much an authoring vehicle (although it was widely thought to be one for a long time), but simply a very efficient "toolbox" used to arrange multidisciplinary information in a hypertext environment. Hypertext programming is not simple—also contrary to popular belief—but using a hypercard program is, foremost because of the simplicity and predictability of its access and utility icons. As an additional benefit, Macintosh owners never need to worry about a user's manual when starting up a hypercard-written program: having used one previously, they will be intimately familiar with the user interface of any given hypertext program.

This, regrettably, is not the case in the PC world, where for lack of user interface symbol standards—or even keyboard standards—each new software product usually demands extensive reading of a textbook first. I believe that this factor has been mostly responsible for retarding the growth of digital programming on CD-ROM because CD-ROM was primarily a PC, MS-DOS medium for the first two years of its existence and every search product and piece of published data employed a set of user utilities different from the next. This situation may change in the PC world with the recent introduction of Link software, a hypertext shell developed by IBM for its new PS/2 series computers.

So designing for a digital CD medium has a leg up in the authoring area, but there is a price to pay. Because personal computers—and CD media operate primarily in this area—lack the bandwidth for passing along broadcast video information, making something look like an audiovisual sequence requires power, imagination, and much creativity. For videodisc producers, prescribing a running dialogue between protagonists or animating the mode of action of a given drug is a piece of cake.

Whether one uses DVI or CD-I motion video, it is clear that digital video offers unparalleled digital manipulation possibilities that may, sometime in the future, lead to a new and innovative way of handling video in a PC environment. But this will take time, and I would estimate that the well-proven techniques and sheer experience of the analog videodisc camp will dominate digital design for quite some time.

The reason for this is simple: not many interactive tutorial programs require what I would like to term "virtual video." Virtual video designates an imaginary image, whether still or motion and of finite length, within which the viewer can "roam" about at will. This was never possible with the analog video medium. With analog, if you wanted your viewer to be able to look over his shoulder, you had better include such a video sequence in your shooting script and final program. This is not required for digital video. Given the very large storage capacity of the compact disc (the primary medium at this time, but that may change with the advent of low-cost 3.5" erasable optical disk drives after 1993), one could shoot a video sequence with a 360-degree "fish-eye" lens all the way down, say, Broadway in Manhattan. This very strange video sequence would then be digitized and stored on CD media. Only in actual playback would the fish-eye image be "un-warped" (a favorite term among digital video producers is "warping") giving the viewer the ability to move about in this space, moving his eyes (actually, the video screen in front of him) to the left or right at will, scanning the 360-degree round-about cinemascope image in "unwarped" form.

Sounds ludicrous, or entertaining at best? Not really. Think of the applications for finding your way around hazardous environments like nuclear plants—not to mention the obvious military applications for simulating action on any given European battle "theater." The point is, however, that most interactive training applications today do not require this virtual video sophistication—nor could afford the production cost involved with it. So the virtual video opportunities will be realized only when markets in need of these capabilities—like architectural modelling, interior design, CAD/CAM on a PC, chemical mode-of-action animation, and 3-D clip-art for desktop publishing— are uncovered.

12
Trends

For some 10 years the optical disc industry searched to find its niche in a predominantly magnetic world. Now, at the opening of the 1990s decade, that niche seems to have solidified into a set of technology configurations that utilize optical discs and are rapidly becoming known as "multimedia." The use (and acceptance) of these multimedia/optical media systems by the educational and training markets have been—and will continue to be strongly influenced by developments in the consumer (home and office) marketplace. Consumer-driven trends for home products, such as the wildly successful CD-Audio and the recently introduced combination players, drive trends in the education/training arenas by their effect upon price or consumer acceptance. Consumer-driven trends for office products, fueled by competition between such firms as Microsoft and Apple Computer, will affect education and training in ways that can only be forecast at this time.

Because history often provides clues to future trends, the next section traces the historical trends within the optical disc industry. This was contributed by Jean-pierre Isbouts of Philips and Dupont Optical Company. Dr. Isbouts consistently points out the relationship between the consumer electronic marketplace and the overall optical media industry. The second part of this chapter, written by the author, looks at the trends in education and training that will affect the technology.

* * *

Optical Disc Industry Trends

The Age of the 12-Inch

All through the 70s and early 80s, optical media was a 12-inch business. To benefit from much of the mastering and replication technology that was being developed for Laservision, the first endeavors in the data recordable area also took place on a 12-inch, CAV-formatted disc.

This effort would ultimately culminate in the Megadoc system of Philips, storing 1 gigabyte per side.

And Philips was not the only one. By the time of the 1982 Rothchild Conference on optical media, one of the first dedicated events in the U.S. for the budding industry, there were some 12 companies worldwide developing 12- or 14-inch, 1+ gigabyte subsystems for recordable optical media applications.

Of course, something funny was happening to the world of Laservision at about the same time. Two manufacturers, Pioneer and Sony, had developed drives that included a standard, RS-232 C computer port. This, of course, entertained the possibility of compter-aided videodisc use—not only to enhance computer records with imagery, but also to create a whole new way of interacting with information. This environment allowed you to retrieve information interactively, as with a computer, although this information was not text, but television programming. Naturally, there were not many personal computers around in 1978, and so it took a while before the very novel and fully market-driven concept of computer-controlled interactive videodisc had taken hold. But when it did, Laservision, as a format, had found its niche, and would remain there, riding a slowly growing but steady wave which would ultimately, in 1988, recycle it back into home electronic media.

The Advent of the Compact Disc

If the late 70s had been the era of the 12-inch, the 80s would be dominated by an entirely new format: one that was 5-inch in diameter; one that used the CLV format, which made for slower access but far greater economy of storage; and one which proposed an entirely digital system of information, organized in a system of discrete little units of information called sectors.

Whereas the 12-inch family was a group of media permitted to develop in a relam of relative commercial immaturity, the 5-inch format was the first optical medium to become a commercial—in fact, near-instant success. As a medium to deliver music to the home, it was an astonishing leapfrog into the future—using lasers instead of the century-old technology of stylus and groove, using very high frequency digital sampling of analog waveband, and super-futuristic looking, wafer thin silver discs that, amazingly, carried the entire Ninth Symphony of Beethoven.

The compact audio disc has dramatically changed the way our industry struggled along its path to find broad acceptance for optical technology. Here was a vast success, the most rapidly accepted consumer medium in the history of the modern world—faster than color television or even the VCR. Of course it was limited. It knowingly sacrificed performance—access performance—for greater playing time, but in doing so the CD gave our industry a world standard technology platform where there had been few standards before.

One only has to look at the record of compact disc announcements to understand the fervor which overtook the community and rushed different manufacturers to exploit this ubiquitous compact disc for more elevated—and more lucrative, industrial, professional applications. First, there was CD-ROM.

It took Philips and Sony only two years to agree on a professional standard, using CD technology, that would do no more than maintain the digital information on the disc as data, for computer retrieval use, and not to convert it back to an analog wavelength. Of course, data on such a disc could be anything, and it took an unprecedented effort from several competitive computer manufacturers to agree on a common file and directory standard, popularly known as High Sierra. Long since made an official ISO standard (9660), High Sierra saved the CD-ROM from ignominy it would surely have descended into if it had remained captive to the particular computer—or even software—application.

It did not take long for the hardware community to realize that laserdiscs and CDs had some things in common: they were both read by a laser, for example. And with some changes in rpm and signal processors, it was even conceivable to build players that could play both CDs and laserdiscs. And so, almost despite itself, laser videodisc began the climb to market respectability—riding the crest of consumer demand for ever better, ever more hi-tech CD players. Pioneer, long the lone champion in the U.S. market for consumer laserdisc players, was the first with the so-called "combi(nation) player" class of hardware. Philips, with its U.S. Magnavox and Philips brands, Sony, Marantz, and Panasonic followed.

By 1988 seven different companies had players on the American market (often with different models) ranging from $799 (list) to $1,295 for the truly committed videophiles. Also by 1988, the base of "active" households had risen to 200,000—which was quite respectable. One year later, the installed base had arrived at just below 300,000.

Players had dropped to the $500 level, and retailers were ordering players at a volume of 45 percent over that of 1988.

CD and the Computer Arts

If the CD success can change the way consumers use home video, then perhaps the CD could also provide the platform of innovation for another form of electronic pastime: the home computer and the videogame system. The benefits of a technology carried on a 600 mbyte disc are obvious: software could be richer, with more and better quality graphics, realistic near-CD quality sound effects and even more sophisticated interactivity. All of this, of course, in addition to the same "bonus value" that combi-players offer: when not in use it can always play a nice CD audio disc.

To exploit this opportunity, Philips and Sony developed a separate CD multimedia system called CD Interactive or CD-I; RCA's David Sarnoff Laboratories developed Digital Video Interactive or DVI; SOCS laboratories (admittedly a much smaller manufacturer but with important ties to the toy industry) developed CVD; and finally several home computer and videogame manufacturers have set their first steps with the data storage version of CD Audio: CD-ROM.

And so as we enter the 90s, the second decade of full-fledged optical media developments, there are essentially two main categories of optical media that will lead the assault on magnetic in the business of information distribution. The first is predominantly analog albeit with numerous enhancements developed over the past 10 years. That is the analog laser videodisc, in small (5-inch) or large (8-inch and 12-inch) sizes, with analog or digital (CD-quality) sound. The second is the digital family of compact discs as epitomized by the CD-ROM—5-inch in format and firmly based on developments in consumer electronics.

* * *

Education and Training Trends Affecting Optical Technology

The 1990s Open with Confusion

As this book goes to press, technology proponents in the education and training markets appear to be thoroughly convinced of the educational efficacy of all optical media. Yet at the same time, the predominant trend that has emerged among trainers and educators is one of confusion regarding myriad optical media choices they believe to be available.

Despite the maturation of the videodisc and CD-ROM industries, and the ever-increasing numbers of videodisc and CD-ROM programs, there is a mood of hesitance and caution on the part of educators and trainers regarding optical media and optical curriculum. There is a fear on the part of budgetary decision-makers that current technologies will quickly become obsolete.

The confusion and hesitancy may be attributable to media attention regarding laser-read technologies. Both the professional press and the popular media ran features in the late 1980s that glowingly described new multimedia systems such as DVI in terms that made the media seem imminently and widely available. Further, many articles described futuristic media that do not yet exist, such as *InfoWorld*'s description of "virtual realities," a yet-to-be-invented multimedia in which one, two, or several people can wear "eyephones" that let them "see" and even move through a computer-generated world (Johnston, 1989). As early as February 1987 (in an article ostensibly devoted to videodisc training) *Newsweek* was alerting readers to NASA's prototype "artificial reality" helmets which have 3-D television screens and stereo speakers inside the helmet.

Gery (1989, p. 46) captured the uncertainty of trainers in the corporate world in the late 1980s when she wrote, "New technologies are complex and constantly changing. It seems risky even to invest time to learn about them, let along bring them into a company to meet specific training needs." Danny Hupp, of Pittsburgh-based Partners in Change, reported that by mid-1989, half of all questions directed toward him at corporate training conferences concerned CD-ROM (Geber, 1989). And from the educational world, Professor Blodget of California Polytechnic University at San Luis Obispo commented that many educators who view Apple Computer's multimedia videos believe that futuristic technologies (talking computers) featured in those videos will soon be commercially available.

Ironically the trends toward confusion and hesitancy are occurring at a time when optical technology for education and training has achieved a respectable maturity.

Previously, videodisc technology was severely restricted by the lack of portability of courseware. Yet since early 1988, the Interactive Video Industry Association (IVIA) has been working to develop recommendations to alleviate courseware portability problems. IVIA's Compatibility Committee is working with manufacturers, applications developers, and users to arrive at a solution which reduces the problems of videodisc systems incompatibility. For additional information on the IVIA Compatibility Committee, contact IVIA, 1900 L Street N.W., Suite 500, Washington, D.C. 20036 (202) 872-8845.

Many sources believe that IBM's InfoWindow has already become the defacto standard for industrial and corporate training. InfoWindow was further strengthened in 1989 by Sony's release of the VIW-5000 which emulates InfoWindow. Visage also offers an upgrade system that enables users to run most courseware developed for IBM's InfoWindow.

At the same time Apple's Hypercard program for the Macintosh has spurred videodisc projects at an ever accelerating rate—especially in higher education. And for the lower-cost computers typically used in public education, authoring programs such as TutorTech for the Apple IIs and HyperStudio for the Apple IIGS give educators the ability to tailor the numerous videodisc programs to their district's curriculum. IBM's LinkWay authoring program will likewise extend the use of videodisc curriculum for educators using IBM or MS-DOS compatible computers.

Videodisc courseware for both corporate and public education is reaching what David Hon long ago called "the critical mass." There are at least 450 off-the-shelf courses for InfoWindow, and Ztek's 1989 catalog lists almost 250 videodiscs suitable for education.

Overall, optical publishing is growing rapidly. It is expected that by the end of 1989, there will be up to 400 CD-ROM titles. And while there are currently few CD-ROM programs fashioned into traditional curriculum, there are educational uses for the large volumes of information already available on CD-ROM. Researchers in higher education and the corporate world will be able to make discoveries or analyses heretofore impossible. For example, by accessing a large volume of weather data distributed by the University of Washington on CD-ROM, professors at UCLA were able to discover new radiation patterns.

A strong foundation (hardware- and software-based) exists to support this generation of optical media in education and training. And as was pointed out in Dr. Isbouts' section, the growth in the consumer marketplace for laser-read media strongly supports complementery growth in education and training.

But it is not yet possible to determine whether the hesitancy and confusion concerning which generation of optical hardware/software is the safest investment will abate by itself, or whether the uncertainty will have to be redressed via concerted attention from educators, trainers, and optical industry professionals. That uncertainty can potentially affect all other trends (hardware, courseware, monetary, etc.) as the 1990s dawn.

13
The Industry's Commitment to the Future

I nteractive optical technology's current, box-linked configurations (computers, videodisc players, CD-ROM drives, monitors) will be transitory. Eventually all effects—text, graphics, sound, still images, and moving images—will be handled by the computer. The computer will handle these varied media as it now handles text and graphics. The ultimate integration, "multimedia," will occur inside the computer.

The optical industry's powerful constituencies (hardware and courseware firms, as well as professional associations) are making substantial investments in current optical technologies—and to their converging "multimedia" descendants of the future. Almost daily there are announcements that foretell the multimedia desktop workstation. This chapter will discuss the commitments that key players are making to the interactive optical industry's future.

Manufacturers

Apple Computer, Inc. has made multimedia a major focus and has established a research and development lab expressly devoted to multimedia in San Francisco. The lab is developing such products as "Visual Almanac," an interactive multimedia demonstration kit that combines videodisc and the Macintosh personal computer with Hypercard. That information product is the result of two years of research with children and educators to determine how interactive technologies can best create multi-sensory environments that address different learning styles. "What the multimedia lab team is doing is creating 'design examples' that will demonstrate how multimedia products can be integrated into both education and business" (McCarthy, 1989).

Other Apple-sponsored multimedia products likewise denote the firm's commitment to the interactive optical media industry. For example a "Custom Developer Sampler" CD-ROM disc was developed by Apple's Business Multimedia Group. That disc is targeted to the custom developer and consultant communities, publishers, and Apple field sales, and is designed to assist them in the development of business multimedia projects. Apple has also announced the availability of Media Control Architecture, a suite of protocols and device drivers for use in creating multimedia applications.

Apple is also encouraging third-party development including traditional Mac developers, as well as its new partners in the information business, to use multimedia technology to create new, different applications. Jean-Louis Gassee, president of Apple Products, says that Apple is working with developers to better present information through video images and sound. At the MacWorld Boston'89, six information providers (Datapro, Harvard University, ABC News Interactive, WGBH, Newsweek and Warner Audio) demonstrated how multimedia applications can access graphic and video images from a videodisc or sound from a CD player. "Today we are seeing the dream of multimedia turning into product reality. . .," said Apple CEO John Sculley in his keynote address at the conference.

IBM's education division has announced that multimedia will be a primary concern. Speaking of the future of multimedia, IBM's Peter Blakeney asserted, "It is our intent to be a leader." Blakeney explained that IBM will use InfoWindow as a springboard into the multimedia future. He sees very favorable signs of an emerging technology with many uses in non-traditional data processing areas: merchandising products through automated devices; and public information distribution in such locations as city, county, or state offices, or 24-hour information outlets as in a mall.

Of particular importance to the future of multimedia is the IBM/Intel/Microsoft trinity. IBM President of Entry Systems Division James Cannivino announced at Microsoft's Fourth International Conference on CD-ROM that IBM will codevelop Digital Video Interactive (DVI) systems with Intel. Cannivino also announced at that time that IBM will cooperate with Microsoft to provide open standards and also complete hardware and software systems for DVI, including support in OS/2 Presentation Manager and Windows/386. Together, those three firms—IBM, Intel, and Microsoft—represent significant investments in the joint development of DVI multimedia products.

Microsoft, IBM, and Intel expect their products (based on CD-ROM/XA and Digital Video Interactive) to become the standard multimedia platform by the mid-1990s. *Infoworld* reported that the first multimedia-capable machines will be shipped in 1990 and 1991 (Johnston, 1989). Those will be 386SX-based PCs with enhanced VGA graphics, digital signal processing (DSP) chips, and built-in CD ROM/XA drives.

In conjunction with this effort, Microsoft has established a multimedia division and formed a new multimedia publishing group (formerly Microsoft Press group) which produces information-driven CD-ROM titles. Microsoft also has a new systems group which will provide software platforms and authoring tools for applications developers. Rick Hargrove, group program manager for multimedia systems, stated that Microsoft will enhance Windows/386 and OS/2 with new applications programming interfaces (APIs) to support audio devices, animation support, data transfer, and timing services, as well as search and rich text display engines.

For the IBM-compatible multimedia market to become profitable, a number of trends have to converge. First, a commercially viable market for CD-ROM developers must be nurtured. William Gates of Microsoft estimates that an installed base of at least one million CD drives is needed for a commercially viable market for software developers (Johnston, 1989). The second convergence must be the introduction of a home computing platform based on CD ROM/XA. Also important, prices must come down considerably—less than $1,000 for the home market.

Computer hardware vendors other than Apple and IBM are also supporting multimedia. Commodore's Amiga is entering the field as a workstation contender for the delivery of multimedia. Widely advertised by Commodore for its "superior graphics," an Amiga videodisc system can be assembled for less than $4,000.

The manufacturers of videodisc hardware have also made considerable investments in the future of these various media. Pioneer Communications' manufacturing facility in Carson, CA (which currently has a capacity of 300,000 discs a month) will double its capacity in the near future according to Barbara Zediker, Pioneer's Western Regional Software Sales Manager. Pioneer's newest videodisc player, the LD-V2200, was introduced especially for the educational marketplace. The features of that player are those that have been identified as most important to have in a classroom-based videodisc player. The price of $895 is affordable for most educational institutions, whether K-12 or higher education.

Another major videodisc hardware vendor has been broadening its possible market base as well. Sony's VIW-500, which was introduced at the 1989 Orlando SALT Conference, features IBM InfoWindow emulation. This system costs $4,995—in contrast to more than $8,000 for other systems in Sony's View Line. This makes the SONY VIW-500 affordable to many more training departments in smaller businesses.

The CD-I multimedia configuration is also receiving considerable investment and commitment. Philips and Dupont Optical Company, Sony, and Matsushita are manufacturers working to bring CD-I to market. Philips has lined up 25 titles for CD-Interactive, chiefly games and electronic reference works including a create-your-own music video program, and multimedia versions of golf, casino games, and Clue. The consumer CD-I will be available for June/July 1990 in targeted markets. The product launch will be supported by an extensive consumer awareness campaign focusing on demonstrations and events marketing with displays at trade shows, expos, and theme parks.

Commitment to multimedia technologies can come in forms other than hardware/courseware development. For example Philips and Dupont Optical Media Company has created a "Creative CD-ROM Applications Awards" program which will recognize outstanding achievements with that medium. All entries for the awards program will be judged by an independent panel of judges on the basis of creativity and commercial benefit and their ability to demonstrate expanded applications of optical storage and distribution technology. One Grand Prize Winner and two Honorable Mentions will be announced at the 1990 Microsoft International Conference on CD-ROM. After the awards are granted Philips and Dupont Optical will mount a major publicity effort aimed at gaining broad exposure for winning applications.

Professional Associations

Well-organized groups of professionals representing both end-users and developers of optical technologies are fast gaining strength and influence as the 1990s approach. These types of organizations allow interested professionals to pool their talents and resources to better further the use of interactive optical technologies.

The Optical Publishing Association (OPA), constituted in September 1988, is a trade association dedicated to the development and promotion of the optical publishing enterprise. The three purposes of the OPA are to: 1) promote and encourage the development of digital optical publishing; 2) educate the public about the benefits and applications of optical publishing technology; and 3) serve as a conduit for the exchange of information, opinions, and analysis within the optical publishing industry and new technological developments.

The Interactive Video Industry Association (IVIA) was formed as a vehicle for developing the interactive video market. By mid-1989 the IVIA had more than 150 members—all with interests in multimedia. In line with its goal to achieve broadly supported industry practices that will alleviate courseware portability problems, the IVIA has been sponsoring a Compatibility Committee. The IVIA has been working with manufacturers, applications developers, and users to arrive at a solution which significantly reduces the problems of IVD systems incompatibility. David Shefrin, the IVIA's 1989 chairman, wrote that the organization's goals are the following:

1. Keep the general public as well as specific interest groups informed about the success and promise of interactive video.
2. Distinguish the laser videodisc as a viable, proven option to solve problems in learning and training compared with other seemingly competitive technologies.
3. Persuade the public that videodisc holds good future promise for electronic publishing activities that will serve work, home, school, library, museum, and other settings where visual information has a place.

IVIA's Tech 2000 gallery, a showcase for interactive technology, will open in late 1989 at the Techworld Plaza in Washington, D.C. The gallery is positioned to provide a high-profile center for the display and interpretation of emerging information technologies. This type of visibility in the nation's capital will be especially helpful for optical industry professionals attempting to communicate the technology's capabilities to educational/political policy makers.

A third major professional organization encouraging the growth of optical technologies is the International Interactive Communication Society (IICS). It is an association of communication industry professionals dedicated to the advancement of interactive video and related technologies. IICS affords a forum where individual professionals interested in optical media can band together with larger firms for the development of the multimedia markets.

Despite all the commitment on the part of optical media organizations and professionals, a great many problems remain to be solved. The May 1989 *Interactive Industry News* lamented, "after ten years of activity in the U.S., there is little general public identification of inter-active video as a useful and successful tool for education and commu-nications. . . ."

A great many questions also remain to be answered. What will it take to bring multimedia to the end-user market? What are the most appropriate distribution channels? What sort of training and support will multimedia products require? What procedures are necessary to secure rights to materials not in the public domain?

This chapter has described the efforts of the key players in the op-tical industry. Concerted, continued commitment will be necessary to bring widespread public acknowledgment that interactive multimedia are useful and successful tools for education and communications.

14
Optical Technologies Meet Societal Needs

T he education and training markets for interactive optical technologies have been and will continue to be profoundly affected by a
changing world and economy. Structural shifts such as the growth of
service industries, technological advances in computers and electronics, and global social problems that include overpopulation, hunger
and human rights, have created demands for highly educated citizens
and workers. The globalization of the economy now renders trained
intelligence—human capital—a nation's greatest asset.

This chapter will discuss these and other societal changes and
their resultant education and training needs that can be addressed by
optically based curriculum.

Societal Changes Requiring Educational Redress

The educational skills individuals need to become productive workers
and citizens have already increased and will continue to increase dramatically both now and into the next century. There has been a significant rise in the standard of literacy skills required of the general population. The educational standards currently being applied across the
population have in the past been limited to those interested in postsec-
ondary education as opposed to entry-level employment after completion of high school. Until recently the literacy criteria for the general
population involved the ability to answer questions, follow directions,
and derive meaning from relatively simple texts. Now societal and
workplace expectations require that students and workers develop sophisticated skills that include the ability to a) comprehend a wide
range of familiar and unfamiliar texts; b) communicate effectively
both orally and in writing; c) think critically and reason logically; and
d) solve problems and make decisions (National Academy of Sciences,
1984; National Commission on Excellence in Education, 1983). Projec-

tions indicate that by the 1990s anyone who reads below a 12th-grade level will be excluded from employment.

Yet while the literacy requirements are rising, the literacy level of our general population is declining. Current estimates indicate that the number of functional illiterates in our country is increasing by approximately 2.25 million persons each year. In a concept document from Howard University and New York Institute of Technology's Center for Communications, Learning and Technology, Cheek and Taylor (1988, p. 13) warned that a "permanent underclass of illiterates who are uneducated, untrainable and economically dependent may develop" if current illiteracy trends continue unabated.

Low educational achievement on a large scale, though never desirable, could be tolerated in a largely farming or industrial economy. In an information-based economy, low educational achievement over the long term means declining societal and individual standards of living leading to a failure to remain competitive in a global economy. Terrell Bell, former Secretary of Education, also warned, "It hasn't sunk into the psyche of America, and into the minds of our people, that this dreadful problem is going to destroy us if we don't learn to cope with it more effectively than we have."

Curricula of any kind is a planned series of events designed to have educational consequences for the learner. Optically based curriculum has certain strengths (interactivity, individualized, emulation of human thinking) that can be utilized to meet many of the educational needs caused by societal changes. The following two sections describe education and training needs caused by the aforementioned societal shifts and give examples of ways interactive optical curriculum can be (or has been) designed to meet those needs.

Formal Education

The increasing demand for a highly literate population is placing a great deal of pressure on the traditional educational system—which is faced with numerous internal and external dilemmas. The following major shifts occurring within formal education can be met educationally with appropriately designed optical curricula:

- the increasing numbers of "at risk" students
- the increase in non-English speaking students
- the teacher shortage

"At Risk" Students

More and more students are categorized today as "at risk." That term refers to a student who is in danger of failing to complete her education with an adequate level of skills. Risk factors include low achievement, retention, behavior problems, poor attendance, low socioeconomic status, and attendance at schools with large numbers of poor students.

Slavin and Madden (1989) analyzed "at risk" programs and found that effective programs are comprehensive (include teacher's manuals and supportive materials), intensive (one-to-one) and frequently assess student progress in order to adapt instruction to individual needs.

Educators and budgetary decision-makers considering multimedia curriculum must avoid the stratification that typifies computer use in schools today. Surveys of computer use reveal that in schools with large "at risk" populations computers are used primarily to provide basic-skills instruction delivered by drill-and-practice software. Conversely, computer use in majority schools emphasizes the use of computers as tools to develop higher order literacy and cognitive skills (Center for the Social Organization of Schools, 1983-84; Shavelson, Winkler, Stasz, Feibel, Robyn, & Shana, 1984).

Limited-English-Speaking Students

Classrooms today are populated with students from diverse backgrounds who bring a greater variety of languages, values, and abilities than ever before. Large numbers of students speak minimal or no English. The Los Angeles School District already has students who speak 81 different languages.

Multilingual curriculum is needed and the various optical media provide many modalities in which to deliver the instruction: video, audio, text, and graphics. Once again, past experience offers guidelines to future developers and purchasers of optically based language curriculum. Language is learned most easily when the teaching/learning exercises are whole, functional, and meaningful. Designers and purchasers of multimedia language materials must avoid materials that teach language in bits and pieces, with undue emphasis on isolated aspects.

The Computer Assisted Language Learning and Instruction Consortium (CALICO) is the established leader in the research and development of multimedia learning materials. Readers interested in exploring the topic in depth may contact CALICO, 3078 JKHB, BYU, Provo, UT 84602.

Teacher Shortage

America will need to replace one million teachers before the end of the century, but only eight percent of today's 1.6 million college freshmen are interested in teaching—and only half of those are likely to actually go into the profession.

The teacher shortage will result in more students per classroom and more students per teacher—students who will be in serious need of individual attention. At the same time the teacher will be in critical need of assistance—assistance which can be provided by well-designed multimedia courseware.

As the current generation of teachers retires, colleges of education have an unprecedented opportunity to introduce large numbers of new teachers to educational technologies—including interactive optical technologies. It should be easier to introduce technology usage to teacher trainees than to change the practices of teachers who have been in the classrooms for years.

While formal education is facing its dilemmas, corporate education and training programs also have distinctive needs caused by societal shifts.

Corporate Education and Training

Three major shifts and their resultant training needs which the optical media industry can address are as follows:

- the growth of service sector jobs and their requisite demand for *technological expertise*
- the growth in the number of jobs that demand a higher level of *basic literacy skills*
- the growth in the number of jobs that demand higher-level *reasoning/problem-solving* skills on the part of workers

Training for Technological Expertise

"Videodisc cannot be surpassed in its ability to provide training simulations" (Isbouts, 1989). Videodisc-based simulations of on-the-job tasks and their requisite sequences can provide learners with a close approximation of the actual activity. For example a welding trainee can "pre-experience" the use of welding equipment with Ixion's videodisc program which lets the trainee light and adjust an oxyacetylene torch on the system's monitor.

From the employer's standpoint, optical media's simulations reduce the risk and cost of trainee's errors. Ford Motor Company's Technical Training Section's Don Robbins stressed this feature when discussing Ford's use of InfoWindow for training, "Even if a student makes a mistake, we don't run the risk of damaging a very expensive piece of machinery" (Schneider, 1989).

Optical media's ability to provide simulated training is especially valuable today and for the future in light of the rapid growth of service sector jobs and high-technology industries (and the demise of heavy manufacturing industries).

Since 1980 the labor force has lost five million blue-collar jobs while witnessing the rapid expansion of service occupations such as secretaries, legal assistants, and financial advisors (Bastian, Fruchter, Gittell, Grett & Haskins, 1985). Within these service occupations more and more tasks require technological expertise—which requires training. In fact, Lusterman's 1988 "Trends in Corporate Education and Training" report indicated that technological change has been the principal—often the sole—force behind new training needs for nonmanagerial and technical personnel.

These nonmanagerial and technical personnel groups often represent sizable numbers of employees performing the same tasks. Developers of videodisc courseware are moving to develop training programs for certain larger generic markets, such as office workers. For example IBM's 1989 "InfoWindow Courseware Guide" lists 20 videodisc programs produced by Comsell, Inc. which teach such computer programs as Lotus 1-2-3, WordPerfect, WordStar, and Symphony.

Another example of videodisc programs for training markets with sizable populations are the industrial skills programs marketed by Applied Learning. Oscilloscopes, multimeters, basic electronic components, basic troubleshooting, are but a few of the 29 subjects listed in Applied Learning's "Integrated Curriculum Planner."

Training for Literacy

The demographics of a shrinking work force—characterized by minimal or inadequate academic skills—have forced businesses to institute educational programs designed to teach workers basic skills in reading, writing, and computation.

Optical media software offers a major advantage to employers in that customized courseware can be developed in such a way that it "contextualizes" literacy skills to a specific workplace. Not only is such customization economically efficient for employers (in that employees can learn the exact vocabulary or mathematical calculations necessary for the specific job), but it is also pedagogically correct. Lauren Resnick and Leopold Klopfer, co-directors of a major center for research on cognition and learning, emphasize the importance of subject matter and situation-specific instruction (1989).

An excellent example of customization and "contextualization" is the Domino's Pizza videodisc. Under a U.S. Department of Labor Grant, Domino's Pizza contracted with Educational Data Systems, Inc. to develop a videodisc program designed to teach literacy skills to Domino's dough-making staff. Entitled "Vincent Van Dough" (and starring cartoon character Vincent Van Dough), the program is designed to teach employees how to make dough by understanding the written instructions and the mathematical measurements involved in the process.

Training for Reasoning/Problem-Solving Skills

Interactive optical courseware has significant interactive characteristics that can be harnessed to emulate human thinking in order to meet the "upskilled" reasoning/problem-solving skills already being demanded by today's workplace—with heightened demand for those skills in tomorrow's work arenas. According to a recent study conducted by the American Society for Training and Development (ASTD) and the United States Department of Labor, future training programs will have to add components that develop employees' competence in creative thinking, learning how to learn, problem solving, interpersonal relations, and working in teams.

Federal Express' use of interactive videodisc programs which incorporate simulation-based problem scenarios designed to actively involve the company's line of aircraft maintenance personnel in the learning process is an excellent example of the use of optical technologies to teach reasoning skills (Tuttle, 1988).

It is in these final pages that the true worth of interactive optical technologies in education and training is broached. A good curriculum will emphasize the values, sentiments, knowledges, and skills that provide a society with stability and vitality and individuals with the motivation and inner controls of conduct. We can expect and accept no less from interactive optical curricula.

Appendix: Firms and Organizations

Allen Communication
140 Likeside Plaza II
5225 Wiley Post Way
Salt Lake City, UT 84116
801/537-7800

Annenberg/CPB
1111 Sixteenth Street NW
Washington, D.C. 20036
202/955-5241

Apple Computer
20525 Mariani Avenue
Cupertino, CA 95014
408-996-1010

Applied Learning
1751 West Diehl Road
Naperville, IL 60540
312/369-3000

Computer Assisted Language Learning & Instruction Consortium
(CALICO)
3078 JKHB , Brigham Young University
Provo, UT
801/387-7079

Comsell, Inc.
500 Tech Parkway
Atlanta, GA 30313
404/872-2500

Education Systems Corporation
617 Cornerstone Court, Suite 300
San Diego, CA
619-587-0087

EmTech Education Corporation
2401 Colorado Avenue
Santa Monica, CA 94040
213/829-7141

Euro Coordination—IBM
Tour Pascal—LaDefense
F-92075, Paris La Defense
France
47676408

Healthcare Interactive Videodisc Consortium
c/o Paula O'Neill
Instructional Resources, University of Texas
M.D. Anderson Center
Houston, TX
713/792-6730

IBM
Multimedia Solutions
P.O. Box 2150
Atlanta, GA 30055

ICD Corporation
c/o Burl Woodbury
750 N. 200 W., Suite 302
Provo, UT 84601

IMC
100 Fifth Avenue
Waltham, MA 02154
617/890-7707

Information Access Company
11 Davis Drive
Belmont, CA 94002
800/227-8431

Interactive Video Industry Association
1900 L. Street, N.W.
Suite 500
Washington, D.C. 20036

McGraw-Hill, Inc.
1221 Avenue of the Americas
New York, NY 10020
212/337-5962

Partners in Change
Summerfield Village
2547 Washington Road, Suite 720
Pittsburgh, PA 15241
412/854-5750
Danny Hupp

Philips & DuPont Optical Co.
1409 Foulk Road, Suite 200
Wilmington, DE 19803
302/479-2507

Pioneer Communications of America
600 East Crescent Avenue
Upper Saddle River, NJ 07458
201/327-6400

Rediffusion Simulation, Inc.
2200 Arlington Downs Road
Arlington, TX 76011
817/640-5000

Sandy Corporation
1500 West Big Beaver Road
Troy, MI 48084
800/521-5378

Silverplatter Information, Inc.
37 Walnut St.
Wellesley Hills, MA 02181
617/239-0306

Sony Corporation of America
MD-3-17 Sony Drive
Park Ridge, NJ 07656
201/930-6177

Spectrum
9 Oak Park Drive
Bedford, MA 01730
617/271-0500

Systems Impact
200 Girard Street
Suite 211
Gaithersburg, MD 20877
301/869-0400

Teaching Technologies
P.O. Box 3808
San Luis Obispo, CA 93403-3808
805/541-3100

Videodisc Monitor
P.O. Box 26
Falls Church, VA 22046-0026

Videodiscovery
P.O. Box 85878
Seattle, WA 98145
206/285-5400

VideoLogic
245 First Street
Cambridge, MA 02142
617/494-0530

Visage, Inc.
1881 Worcester Road
Framingham, MA 07101
617/620-71**(is it 00?)

Wilson Learning
7500 Flying Cloud Drive
Eden Prairie, MN 55344
612/828-8828

Ztek
P.O. Box 1968
Lexington, KY 40593
800/252-7276

Glossary

access time: The amount of time it takes a computer or keypad device to access information on an optical storage disc and display the information on a monitor.

artificial intelligence: The capability of a computer-directed device to perform functions that are normally associated with human intelligence, such as reasoning, learning, and self-improvement.

authoring software: Computer software program that allows a designer to write organizational schemes with which to direct a viewer's path through an optical courseware program.

authoring system: Prepackaged courseware templates of menu-driven editors designed to help authors create courseware without elaborate programming.

branching: An instruction to diverge from one frame on a video-disc program to another frame.

CAV (constant angular velocity) laserdisc: laser videodisc format; holds 54,000 frames, each of which can be addressed and presented individually. Thirty minutes of linear video.

CLV (constant linear velocity) laserdisc: Unable to display specific frames—with the exception of Pioneer's new LDV-8000 player. Sixty minutes of linear video.

Compact-Disc Interactive (CD-I): Optical technology that can handle data from a variety of source media, can store up to 650 MB, over 7,800 video still frames, more than two hours of top-quality sound, 17 hours of simple narration, and up to 150,000 pages worth of text and graphics.

CD-ROM: Digital storage medium primarily used to store large volumes of reference materials or abstracts. Can store equivalent of: contents of 1,200 5.25 floppy disks, 5,000 real-life images, and text to 150,000 pages. Digitally stores still-frame video, audio, date, and computer code in any combination.

CD-XA: Incorporates audio and graphics technology from the CD-I format and serves as a bridge between CD-ROM and CD-I.

curriculum: A series of planned events that are intended to have educational consequences for one or more students.

Digital Video Interactive (DVI): Uses digital compression and decompression to store 72 minutes of full-screen, full-motion video;

can work with any digital medium—including CD-ROM, hard disk, or WORM.

Healthcare Interactive Videodisc Consortium: A group of 17 medical and nursing schools in the United States and Canada developing InfoWindow-compatible videodisc instruction for healthcare training.

industrial training: Development of nonmanagerial, technical, and non-technical skills in industry.

InfoWindow: IBM's multimedia presentation system that consists of an InfoWindow display, an IBM PC or PS/2, the InfoWindow control program, and a videodisc player.

Interactive Video Industry Association (IVIA): The non-profit industry organization representing the interessts of companies and organizations involved in the creation, use, and marketing of interactive video and multimedia computing technology. (Address: 1900 L. Street, N.W., Suite 500, Washington, D.C. 20036.)

interactivity: A reciprocal dialogue between the learner and the program.

laser: Light amplification by stimulated emission of radar.

multimedia: refers to systems that integrate video, text, and graphics by combining a computer with an optical technology peripheral.

NTSC: The color standard established by the American National Television Standards Committee. Used in America, Canada, Japan, the Bahamas and Philippines. NTSC uses a 525-line screen with 30 frames per second.

optical technology: Based on the principle that information can be translated—via a laser beam—into physical impressions on a disc. Those physical impressions can later be read back—and decoded into video, text, graphics, and audio.

PAL: Television and video color standard developed in West Germany and used in the United Kingdom, throughout most of Europe, Africa, Australia, and South America. Uses a 625-line screen, with 25 frames per second.

professional education: Develops a breadth of knowledge in the theoretical constructs upon which the learner is to synethsize and later draw upon when making autonomous decisions in the workplace. Does not emphasize specificity or sequenced behavior

repurposing: a process that uses authoring software for the creation of a computer program that accesses a videodisc's audio and visual frames. Can include the inclusion of text and graphics.

search: To use the computer or keypad device to rapidly access information stored on an optical disc.

simulations: Education or training programs that replicate real-life situations (often dangerous or expensive situations). Allow students to experiment with, manipulate, and apply abstract concepts to a situation that proximates reality.

software: Storage media—either optical discs or magnetic disks.

videodisc: Analog storage medium. Produced via process "mastered" with pits (containing audio and video information). A laser beam with TV/video signals that uses laser light to read information from the disc. Information is presented on a standard television or computer monitor.

Bibliography

Bastian, Al, N. Fruchter, M. Gittell, C. Greer, and M. Haskins. *Choosing Equality*. New York: The New World Foundation, 1985.

Peter Blakeney, Telephone Interview. August 1989.

Blodget, Robert. "Ten Uses of Videodisc in Public Schools." *Proceedings for the National Videodisc Symposium for Education*. Lincoln: University of Nebraska, 1987.

————. "Ten Uses of Videodisc in Public Schools." *Teaching Technologies Newsletter* (January 1989): 2.

Dori Bower, Telephone Interview, June 26, 1989.

Bowers, Richard. *Optical Publishing Directory*. Medford, NJ: Learned Information, Inc., 1988.

Brownstein, Mark. "Multimedia Still Awaits Definition." *Infoworld* (July 10, 1989): 29.

Carnevale, Anthony. "Management Training: Today and Tomorrow." *Training and Development Journal* (December 1987): 19-29.

Carnevale, Anthony, and Eric Schulz. "Technical Training in America: Who Much and Who Gets It?" *Training and Development Journal* (November 1988): 18-32.

Cassidy, Danny. "Considerations in Marketing Interactive Videodisc Programs to Hospitals." *Medical Disc Reporter* 4 (2) (March-April 1988).

Center for the Social Organization of Schools. *School Uses of Microcomputers: Reports from a National Survey*. Baltimore, MD: Johns Hopkins University, 1983-84.

Cheek, King, and Orlando Taylor. *Concept Document for Joint Center for Communications, Learning, and Technology*. Howard University and New York Institute of Technology, 1988.

Cohen, Vicki Blum. "Utilizing Interactive Features in the Design of Videodisc Materials." Paper presented at American Educational Research Associaiton (Montreal, Canada, April 11-14, 1983).

Comcowich, William. "The Future of Videodisc, and Expert Systems in Medical Education." *Proceedings for Second Annual Conference on Learning Technology in the Health Care Sciences*. Warrenton, VA: SALT, 1987.

Daynes, R. *The Videodisc Book: A Guide and Directory.* New York: John Wiley and Sons, 1984.

DeBloois, M. *Effectiveness of Interactive Videodisc Training: A Comprehensive Review.* Falls Church, VA: Future Systems Incorporated, 1984.

Emerson, Lou. "Can Computers Answer America's Training Needs?" *Instruction Delivery Systems* (January/February 1988): 10-12.

Evans, Alan. "Videodisc Produced at University Helps Teachers Study Discipline Situations." *Inside* (February 1987): 1.

Feuer, Dale. "*Training* Magazine's Industry Report 1988." *Training* (October 1988): 31-34.

Geber, Beverly. "Whither Interactive Videodisc?" *Training* (March 1989): 47-49.

Gery, Gloria. "Interactivity: The Heart of the CBT Matter." *Proceedings: 1989 Interactive Instruction Delivery.* Warrenton, VA: SALT, 1989.

Gordon, Jack. "Who is Being Trained To Do What?" *Training* (October 1988): 51-60.

Harney, John. "A Comparison of Different CD-ROM Local Area Networks in Universities." *CD-ROM End User* (June 1989): 17.

————. "Medline on CD-ROM." *CD-ROM End User* (June 1989): 9-10.

Helgerson, Linda. "The CD-ROM Industry at the 4 1/2 Year Mark." *CD Data Report* (April 1989): 17-21.

Hiscox, Michael. "Integrating Testing and Instruction Using the Videodisc." Paper presented to the Annual Conference of the Society for Applied Learning Technology (Los Angeles, CA, August 1981).

Hodgkinson, Harold. "The Right Schools for the Right Kids." *Educational Leadership* (February 1988): 10-15.

Hoelscher, Karen. "Evaluating Interactive Video at Harvard Law School." *The Videodisc Monitor* (August/September 1988): 39.

Hoffos, Signe. "Update on Interactive Video in Britain and Europe." *Optical Information Systems,* 1988.

Holmberg, Borje. "On the Concept and Academic Discipline of Adult Education." ERIC ED 290 010.

Johnston, Stuart. "IBM, Intel Codeveloping DVI Multimedia Products." *Infoworld* (April 3, 1989).

Jones, T. "Dovetailing Chunks: A Technique for the Optimizing of Interactive Videodisc Design." *T.H.E Journal* 16(2) (1988): 90-94.

Kirchner, G. "Simon Fraser University VIdeodisc Project: Part One: Design and Production of an Interactive Videodisc for Elementary School Children." *Videodisc/Videotext* 2(4) (1982): 275-287.

Kirchner, G. "Simon Fraser University Videodisc Project: Part

Two: Field Testing of an Interactive Videodisc for Elementary School Children." *Videodisc/Videotext* 3 (10) (1983): 45-58.

Sandi Kirshner, Telephone Interview, June 15, 1989.

Debbie Kirtland, Telephone Interview, July 1989.

Kurz, Maxwell. *Ztek's Interactive Videodiscs & CD-ROM for Education*. Lexington, Ky.: Ztek, 1989.

Landro, Laura. "Get Set for Laser Videodisks, Round Two." *The Wall Street Journal* (December 6, 1988): B8.

Lee, Chris. "Training Budgets: Neither Boom Nor Bust." *Training* (October 1988): 41-46.

Lewis, Martina. *Videodiscs for English Classes*. Marina del Rey, Calif.: Probata Press, 1989.

Lubin, David. "Building Performance Systems of the Future." In *Proceedings of February, 1989 Interactive Instruction Delivery*. Warrenton, Va.: Society for Applied Learning Technology, 1989.

Lusterman, Seymour. "Trends in Corporate Education and Training." ERIC ED 296 083, 1988.

McCarthy, Robert. "Multimedia, What the Excitement's All About." *Electronic Learning* (June 1989): 26-31.

McNeil, Donald. "Technology is a Hot Topic, But Its Impact on Higher Education Has Been Minimal." *The Chronicle of Higher Education* (June 7, 1989): A44.

Miller, Rockley. "Keynote Address." Society for Applied Learning's 10th Annual Interactive Videodisc in Education and Training Conference, August 24, 1988.

Muller, S. "Physicians for the Twenty-First Century/Report of the Project Panel on the General Professional Education of the Physican and College Preparation for Medicine." *Journal of Medical Education* (November 1984).

Beverly Osteen, Telephone Interview, June 26, 1989.

Parkhurst, Perrin, and Patricia Grauer. "An Interactive Learning Resource Center for Medical Education." *Instruction Delivery Systems* (January/February 1989): 10-22.

Power On!, A Report from the Office of Technology Assessment, Washington, D. C., 1988.

Price, C.L. "Dow Chemical Learns the Challenge of Creating Videodisc-Based Training." *Instruction Delivery Systems* (January/February 1988): 12-14.

Pring, Isobel. "Book Review of 'Nordic Optical Directory.'" *Interactive Media International* (3) (April 1989): 46.

Resnick, Lauren. *Education and Learning to Think*. Washington: National Academy Press, 1987.

Resnick, Lauren, and Leopold Klopfer. "Toward the Thinking Curriculum: An Overview." In *1989 ASCD Yearbook: Current Cognitive Research*. Alexandria, VA: ASCD, 1989.

Rogers, Michael. "Now, Artificial Reality." *Newsweek* (February 9, 1987): 56-57.

Schmidt, Henk, W. Dauphinee, and Vimla Patel. "Comparing the Effects of Problem-Based and Conventional Curricula in an International Sample." *Journal of Medical Education* (62) (April 1987).

Schneider, Barbara. "Interactive Computer System Helping Chase Manhattan Bank Train Tellers in Personalized   Customer Service." *News Release*. Rye Brook, N.Y.: IBM, 1989.

Shavelson, R. J., J.D. Winkler, C. Stasz, W. Feibel, A.E. Robyn, and S. Shana. *Successful Teachers' Patterns of Microcomputer-based Mathematics and Science Instruction*. Report to the National Institute of Education. Santa Monica, Calif.: Rand Corporation, 1984.

Sheingold, Karen, Laura Martin, and Mari Endreweit. "Preparing Urban Teachers for the Technological Future." In *Mirrors of Minds*. Norwood, N.J.: Ablex Publishing, 1987.

Singarella, Thomas. "Videodisc Development in the Health Sciences." *Disctopics* (October 1988).

Singarella, Thomas, Shelly Bader, and Howard Ramagli. "Videodisc Utilization Trends in the Health Sciences." *The Journal of Biocommunication* (Summer 1988): 26-29.

Thomas Singarella, Telephone Interview, University of Tennessee, Memphis, June 1989.

Slavin, Robert, and Nancy Madden. "What Works for Students at Risk: A Research Synthesis." *Educational Leadership* (February 1989): 4-13.

Stewart, Scott Alan. *Videodiscs in Healthcare*. Alexandria, VA: Stewart Publishing, Inc., 1987.

Tobin, J. "Educational Videodisc in Canada." New Technologies in Canadian Education (paper 13). Toronto, Ontario: Educational Communications Authority.

Richard Trynda, Telephone Interview, University of Colorado Health Sciences Center, June 1989.

Tuttle, David. "Federal Express Soars With Quest." *Promptlines* Salt Lake City, Utah: Allen Communications, 1988.

Uhlig, George. *Technological Futures in Education*. ERIC ED, 1982.

Wakeland, Charles. "SLEEPER." *Instruction Delivery Systems* (November/December 1987): 10-13.

West, Peter. "I.B.M. Unveils $25 Million-Dollar Grant Program." *Education Week* (May 10, 1989): 1.

White, Mary Alice. "Implications of the Technologies for Human

Learning." *Peabody Journal of Education*, Beyond the Computer Revolution Special Edition (Summer 1989).

Winters, Doug. "Video, the Power of the Technology." Presentation at IBM-Sponsored Interactive Video: A New Strategy for Leadership Development, DisneyWorld, Florida, February 27, 1989.

Wyer, Jo-Anne, and Charles Findley. "Beneath the Surface: Exploring Interactive Videodisc Gaming Simulation Design for Management Training." Warrenton, VA: Society for Applied Learning Technology, 1985.

Index